To: Dale
Best Wishes
Wayne

"Coach Wimp Sanderson was more than a coach to me. He was like my second father because he made me believe in myself.

I went to the University of Alabama to play basketball as a boy. After four years of playing under him, I left the University of Alabama as a man."

— Gary Waites
A Crimson Tide guard
from 1988 through 1991

Wimp Sanderson and Gary Waites

Plaid and Parquet

An Autobiography By
WIMP SANDERSON

Five Points South Productions

Five Points South Productions

Cover Photography By
Barry Fikes
Tuscaloosa, Alabama

Cover Design By
Melanie Townsend
Portland, Tennessee

Published in Sterrett, Alabama by Five Points South Productions, 7460 Highway 51 South, Sterrett, Alabama 35147

Library of Congress Cataloging-in-Publication Data

Sanderson, Wimp
    Plaid and Parquet/by Wimp
Sanderson — 1st ed.
            p.   cm

ISBN 1-881590-32-1 $27.50
    1. Wimp Sanderson — Autobiography
2. University of Alabama — Basketball — Non-fiction
                            1. Title

Manufactured in the United States of America

*This book is dedicated
to Annette, my wife,
Jim, Scott and Barry, our sons,
and their families.*

Annette and Wimp Sanderson relax with Jim, Scott and Barry at NorthRiver Yacht Club in Tuscaloosa, Alabama

With gratitude to all of the outstanding players I have coached, the two coaches I have served under, my fellow assistant coaches, the assistant coaches who worked under me, our trainers, our managers and our basketball support personnel.

(and)

With thanks to the thousands of loyal fans who diligently supported University of Alabama basketball.

Wimp Sanderson believes great players make coaches successful—and win championships like the Southeastern Conference Tournament

Foreword

Wimp Sanderson is the type of guy who needs a passing lane in a car wash.

That's what I tell people who ask about my buddy, that he's a (Double) A Type individual who's going to get what he wants. In that regard he's like a bulldog who's relentless, a guy who won't stop until he succeeds.

That's the type personality Wimp wielded as a successful college basketball coach, for a decade as significant as anybody in the nation.

We met and started competing as assistant coaches when we were young men. Then we battled tooth and nail as head coaches when I was at Auburn University and he was at the University of Alabama — albeit with integrity a bit contrary to that reserved for most intrastate rivals. Now, as more experienced individuals we host a daily radio show in Birmingham, Alabama.

That longlasting friendship is one reason I'm honored to write a few introductory words about *Plaid and Parquet,* Wimp's auto-biography. I don't have any doubt a reader will find entertaining, humorous and insightful info between the covers.

But to a greater extent I'm delighted because I know anybody who reads this book will consider it a reflection of a colorful and not always easy life.

Wimp says I know him like a book. I don't know if that's totally accurate because he isn't easy to categorize.

But this book is one I'm looking forward to reading — even with the risk he might put a Wimp-like scowl on my smiling face.

—Sonny Smith
Former College Basketball Coach

Foreword

When word surfaced that Wimp Sanderson was writing a book, three questions and answers came to mind.

Will there ever be another coach in the SEC who hated to lose more than my friend Wimp? That is doubtful.

What do you get when you combine a worker and a schemer? A Wimpoholic, because Wimp labored hard as a coach and always looked for an edge for the Alabama program — with game plans, at news media gatherings and in coaches meetings.

What is a pessimist who believes he's going to win? A Wimpster, because Wimp seemed to dread every game, but was ready for action every time he went on stage.

I met Wimp in the early 1960s. We were rookie coaches and big dreamers. In 1966, when I became head coach at Florida State, I tried to hire him as my only assistant. I've had a hand in the recruitment of great players, like Dave Cowens and Dominique Wilkins, but I couldn't get Wimp. He stayed at Alabama and waited for his chance to become head coach. It was a wise choice because 15 years and about 450 games later his big dream came true.

The "Plaid Patroller" did a great job at Alabama because he wouldn't accept anything short of his best effort.

So comes to mind a round of golf. Wimp made an 8-iron shot from 140 yards for an eagle. Most golfers would have been ecstatic. But my loyal friend Wimp quickly said, "I probably won't hit another good shot all day."

That's Wimp, a guy who poor mouths all the way to the bank.

—Hugh Durham
Jacksonville University Basketball Coach

Foreword

I enjoyed playing basketball for Wimp Sanderson, mainly because I enjoyed winning. Coach Sanderson has always been around winning teams and the three years I played for him we made three appearances in the NCAA Tournament Sweet Sixteen and won the SEC regular season championship and the SEC Tournament championship in 1987.

Coach Sanderson demanded my greatest effort every day in every drill the entire time I played for him. He was a smart coach who kept things simple while demanding such effort. I think that's the common thread all of his former players remember, playing as hard as we could every night.

As players we didn't see his humor as much as the rest of the world, but every now and then he would have us laughing hard, at times with him and at times simply because of his personality.

Coach Sanderson did a tremendous job while at the University of Alabama. He was particularly talented developing players. In that regard, Derrick McKey, Keith Askins, Jim Farmer and others come to mind. They made unbelievable progress from their freshman seasons until they became NBA players.

Not only did Coach Sanderson have an enormous impact on University of Alabama basketball, he taught me numerous helpful things I refer to while leading the Crimson Tide program.

— **Mark Gottfried**
University of Alabama Basketball Coach

Plaid and Parquet

INTRODUCTION

From Knickers to Plaid and Parquet

*Wimp and his mother,
Christine, in the 1990s*

*Wimp Sanderson and his father,
Albert, in Florence, Alabama, his
hometown.*

Now that an improbable journey from a modest apartment on a narrow street in Florence, Alabama to a spacious house on a lush golf course at NorthRiver Yacht Club has ended, the time has come for me to share memories from more than three decades as a University of Alabama basketball coach.

After all, a man who spends 38 years coaching, 32 in Tuscaloosa, Alabama, has more than a few triumphant moments and trying times to consider during his retirement.

I hope you will enjoy going back in time with me and remembering some of the joy Alabama basketball and its wonderful players have brought to thousands upon thousands of people in one state and throughout the southeast.

Also, I'm hopeful the book *Plaid and Parquet* will enable me to clear up some misconceptions about my demeanor, my life in general and my career as a coach.

I've been told most people consider me a cantankerous man with zero personality because they've seen me with a horrible scowl on my face during emotional basketball games. That's unfortunate because perception isn't always reality, which is my way of stating I'm not as temperamental as I've appeared to be during the heat of competition.

To be honest, I never knew I didn't smile and I can assure you I didn't intend any harm with that scowl unless it was directed at a referee.

I'm simply a nervous, excitable and competitive person and have been most of my life. Members of my family say I inherited those traits from my grandfather on my daddy's side, Calvin Sanderson, who I can barely remember.

I'm sure a large part of my competitiveness is the result of my childhood, when older and larger boys blistered my fanny with a basketball after rounds of a game we called hot tail. I was overmatched, too small and too frail to meet the challenge, and I'm sure those mornings and afternoons as an underdog helped prepare me for the demands I faced as a coach.

The dreadful scowl might have been permanently put in place after I suffered my first defeat as a basketball coach at Carbon Hill High School. It wasn't easy to smile while staying up three straight nights trying to figure out what went wrong.

Of course, I had a couple of other reasons to frown long before that. My mother made me do two things I utterly despised. She made me take piano lessons from Mrs. Myrtle Roberts, after walking several miles from school at that, and she made me wear knickers to church. I don't remember smiling much on either occasion, nor do I recall practicing much at the piano.

But basketball was different, particularly when I played and coached, because I worked overtime to win and, the truth is, I never learned to handle losing. That has been the case since my one year as a high school coach all the way through to my last loss at the University of Alabama, when North Carolina beat us in the 1992 NCAA Tournament. I won't apologize for that because a fear of failure has driven me since my youth and I think a winner gives up something important when he compromises the desire to be the best.

That drive intensified during the spring of 1980, when I was named University of Alabama head coach after serving 20 years as an assistant coach. I developed an I'll show you and the rest of the world attitude because I knew a lot of people didn't think I deserved the opportunity to lead the program.

Thus surfaced a double edged sword and a more menacing scowl. I never could enjoy the good measure of success we had, a multitude of wins, because I was always fretting over the most recent loss or worrying about the next game.

I've thought about that a lot since 1992, when I coached my last game in the NCAA Tournament.

I've come to realize that's just me, a fierce competitor with a will to win. But that isn't me away from the basketball court, no matter what the majority of people seem to think.

Truthfully, I'm a guy with a wife and three sons who actually smiles a lot when considering the unconventional road I've traveled from childhood to adulthood.

So please allow me to give you a few nuts and bolts about my life, some of the things we'll talk about in this narrative.

My father died when I was six years old and my terrific mother raised me as a single parent.

I met my wife, Annette, as a student at Coffee High School and married her while I was enrolled at Florence State Teachers College, which has become the University of North Alabama. Interestingly, we learned we attended the same kindergarten in East Florence, so I guess it's safe to say we've been partners through most our lives. I can say without doubt she is the most unselfish and understanding person I've known. Together, we've raised three outstanding sons, Jim, Scott and Barry, who have shared the numerous good times and the few bad times we've had as a family.

I've been fortunate to have had superb coaches while playing basketball, to work alongside many great coaches and to coach many outstanding players.

It won't take long for you to realize I'm lucky. I've been in the right place with the right people at the right time — almost always in the nick of time.

While the majority of the credit for what I've accomplished professionally should go to Annette, Jim, Scott and Barry, there are numerous people who have played significant roles in my life.

Hollis Thompson was the principal at Carbon Hill High School who hired me when I had zero experience.

Hayden Riley, an absolutely wonderful person, hired me as a University of Alabama graduate assistant coach.

I got an opportunity to become head coach at the University of Alabama because of Paul "Bear" Bryant, Sam Bailey and, of course, C.M. Newton.

I've seen a lot of faces, some I've liked and some I haven't liked. I've had my share of victories and my share of defeats. I've done a lot of things right and I've done some things wrong. I've competed against famous coaches and rival programs.

For as long as I live I'll never forget the wonderful friends I had during my years in Tuscaloosa. Nor will I forget those devoted Crimson Tide fans who filled Coleman Coliseum. They still talk about memorable victories and heartbreaking losses, some of the same games we'll discuss later.

So how did the *Plaid and Parquet* title for this book evolve?

As Alabama's coach, I was known for wearing resplendent plaid sport coats — and I honestly don't know why I started doing that. Maybe I was trying for a little gusto as a man after my mother forced me to wear knickers to church when I was a child.

The parquet floor Alabama once had in Coleman Coliseum, the home court for basketball games, is a reminder of both my success and failure. At one time it resembled plaid, something different and bedazzling during an exciting time, which was precisely its purpose.

The parquet is gone, having been replaced by a more mundane style of hardwood.

Of course, I've departed, too, which means I'm free to share a lot of good memories with you.

CHAPTER ONE

West Tuscaloosa Street to Tuscaloosa

*Wimp Sanderson continues to have fond memories
of a trip he made as a child to Cleveland, Ohio*

It's a bit paradoxical that I spent my entire childhood, all the way through college, living at 317 West Tuscaloosa Street in Florence, Alabama. To do that and then spend 32 years in Tuscaloosa, Alabama as a University of Alabama basketball coach is a little amusing to me.

But that's how it happened, from West Tuscaloosa Street to Tuscaloosa, and I can say without reservation the later stages of that trip were the most comfortable.

After my father, Albert, died when I was six years old, my mother, Christine, and I lived in a nice one bedroom apartment. We had to share a bath with the people on the other side, which made it fairly inconvenient.

But that's all we could afford, so we got by as best we could, with gratitude to Mary Snow, an understanding landlady who owned the building. Eventually, she added another small room and put another bathroom on the back so we could be more comfortable and I'd have a place to sleep.

My mom was a wonderful person. She worked for the Department of Veteran Affairs. Before I was born she had worked in Washington, D.C. for several dignitaries and had returned to Florence, where she helped military veterans with their pension checks and numerous other forms of paperwork.

Mother lived on West Tuscaloosa Street for 52 years, until she moved to Little Rock, Arkansas with us in 1995. She died in 1998 and I miss her in an unexplainable sort of way.

I don't have many recollections of my dad because he died when I was young and my mom chose not to talk much about the past with me. However, I do recall a day when my dad, my mom and I were riding in an old convertible car with a rumble seat. We had a friendly dog named Boo and, lo and behold, he jumped out of the car and was killed.

Other than that, I've just got a few pictures of my dad and I together. However, I've learned he got an honorable discharge from the U.S. Army and died at age 38 from a heart condition. It's my understanding he left work one afternoon, helped his sisters move some rugs in Sheffield, became ill that evening and died.

So it was just mother and me and she worked extremely hard to make ends meet.

We got a lot of help during those years from Aunt Jo and Uncle Jim White, who looked after me when mom was working. They fed me a lot of meals, picked me up after school and, more or less, took care of me when I needed parental guidance.

I was as close to Aunt Jo and Uncle Jim as anybody in my family. In fact, when they passed away they left a house at 212 West Reader Street in Florence to my mother. When mom died, I became the owner of that house. I've requested that my wife, Annette, and our sons, Jim, Scott, and Barry, never sell the house so it'll always be there as a monument to Aunt Jo and Uncle Jim. It's a special memory of two extraordinary people who helped me through some rough spots growing up.

That doesn't mean I was a bad child. To the contrary, I was a kid who caused few problems. I never drank. I didn't carouse much. About the only thing I did questionable was occasionally thumb rides to a pool room in North Florence just to hang out for a while in a different environment.

I do recall one major fling with mischief that involved a cousin, Joe Hayes Hooks, and me.

We were out in the back yard playing baseball and there was a bee hive just through the hedges. It was a neighborhood fixture that produced a lot of honey for folks up and down the street. But it bothered us to no end and we decided it to get rid of it.

I don't know if it was his idea or mine, but we wadded up some paper, loosely, got some matches and burned down the bee hive.

When my mom got home from work that afternoon, I hurried straight to her and, while wringing my hands, I said, "Mom, I'm in a lot of trouble. We burned down the bee hive."

I don't recall what my punishment was. However, I do know that escapade is a whole lot funnier in retrospect than it was then.

So you can see I was a pretty good boy, to the point I took it like a man when my mother made me wear knickers to church and, gee whiz, take piano lessons after school. To tell you the truth, I don't know which I hated the most, those funny pants or those ridiculous lessons.

I assume it was the piano lessons because they came to mind about four decades later, the day before one of my University of Alabama basketball teams played a game against Tennessee in Knoxville. I remember telling the story to a newspaper columnist and then saying, "But if we beat Tennessee, I'll walk back to Tuscaloosa with a piano on my back and stop and play it every few miles."

We won the game. I flew home with my players.

I took those piano lessons while attending Kilby Training School, a small elementary school on the campus of Florence State Teachers College, which is now the University of North Alabama. I went all six years there and many of my classmates went on to Coffee High School with me.

I got my first taste of sports competition at Kilby Training because we had two kickball teams. One was named the White Panthers and one was named the Black Snakes. Appropriately or not, I was a Black Snake and I asked Aunt Jo to get me a black sweater and embroider black snakes on it. She agreed to do that, which added to my enjoyment of kickball.

To be honest, Kilby Training wasn't known for its academics, but it was a struggle for me to get out of there and advance to junior high school. Years later, several of us joked that we got our elementary school degrees by etching trays, making lanyards and beating on tin cans.

We worked a little harder in the classroom than that, but it was during elementary school years that I received my baptism on the basketball court and you can guess what interested me most.

There was a recreation area around the corner from West Tuscaloosa Street called The Field, I assume because nobody could come up with a more creative name. Anyway, a bunch of older boys played basketball there every day and, naturally, I wanted to join them.

I was small and weak at that time, so I used a grandma shot — heaving the basketball underhanded from between my legs. That's the only way I could get it to the goal, which put me at a major disadvantage.

The older boys liked to play a game called hot tail. It was a version of the standard 21 game kids have played for as long as I can remember. The rules were simple. You got two points for a long shot and one point for a short shot and the first person to land exactly on 21 was the winner.

The difference in hot tail and the standard 21 game is everybody except one player had to score 21 points. The one who didn't score 21, or the last one out, got penalized severely. He had to bend over, grab his ankles and let the other players throw a basketball against his fanny. If you don't think a properly delivered basketball will blister a rear end, ask me about it. I was the little guy who more times than not ended up with the hot tail.

But that's how I fell in love with basketball. I'd play hot tail with the older boys, go home and eat dinner and hurry back to The Field to practice shots by myself. That was after I received my first basketball, a prized possession.

I got that basketball from Sears & Roebuck, straight out of a catalog. I've still got it, as cracked and worn as it is, because I was so proud of it.

The day it arrived I took it to my grandmother's house on West Mobile Street to let her see it. It was a terrible day, cold and rainy, mud on the ground, but it was a rubber basketball I could wash and I was determined to show it off.

Then I took my mail order basketball to The Field and shot it hour after hour day after day.

I was a huge baseball fan, too, and at age 10 that enabled me to take a whirlwind trip most kids can only dream about.

I had an Aunt Fannie who lived in Cleveland, Ohio with her daughter, Virginia Hayes, so I decided I wanted to go up there and watch some Major League Baseball games. Making such a trip at that age isn't an easy thing to do, so I was pleasantly surprised when mother decided to let me go.

The plan was for me to ride a train from Decatur, Alabama to Cincinnati, Ohio, where I'd be met by a traveler's aide who would make sure I made the connecting train to Cleveland.

On the drive from Florence to Decatur, mother was a little nervous and I was a little scared. But she was a thinker and she had a foolproof plan.

First, she pinned a 10-dollar bill to my underwear so I'd have some money on the trip. Then she put a little red comb in my front pants pocket so the traveler's aide would be sure she was meeting the right little blond-haired boy.

The traveler's aide met me in Cincinnati, as planned, took me to a movie so I'd have something to do while waiting for the train to Cleveland and, right on schedule, got me in my seat on the famous Hummingbird.

I thought I was having a perfect trip as we roared along the railroad tracks. What I didn't know is while I had been asleep the train had wrecked and we were behind schedule.

My aunt and her daughter arrived at the train station in Cleveland to pick me up and couldn't find me. Somebody told them they had seen a little blond-haired boy running through the depot screaming out of his mind because he couldn't find his kinfolks. That got them panicky and they stayed that way until somebody told them the Hummingbird was running late.

But all that starts well ends well, or so they say, and I got to watch some great baseball. Bob Feller pitched for the Cleveland Indians. I got to see Larry Doby play his first Major League game. I thought he was the shortstop, but just recently I saw a television interview with him during which he said he played first base. Regardless, I was there when he broke in, even if it took five decades for me to know for sure what positioned he played.

Another special memory from that trip was the series the Indians played against the Boston Red Sox, who had Ted Williams as their star. I wanted his autograph and Aunt Fannie's son, Buddy Barks, thought he could get it for me.

We went down to the Red Sox clubhouse and Buddy, my cousin, asked an attendant if he would go inside and get the autograph. In a flash the man was back with Ted Williams written on a piece of paper. I've always thought something fishy was going on, like maybe somebody else signed the name, because it happened so fast. But I was excited then and to this day I don't know if I've got an authentic Ted Williams autograph.

I stayed in Cleveland three weeks, saw some great players in action and gained all kind of weight. My aunt made pan toast, which was nothing more than fried light bread with a ton of butter on it, and I'd have six or eight slices every time she served it. When I got home, I looked like a little butterball.

Meanwhile, it wasn't long before my bedroom looked like a Cleveland Indians shrine. I got their media brochure, team pictures and cards and filled up an entire wall with them.

Without question, I'd say making that trip to Cleveland, Ohio and feasting on baseball and pan toast was the highlight of my elementary school years.

Basketball became king again during my years at Appleby

Junior High School. In fact, a bunch of classmates and I used to slip over to Bill Ward Roberts' house during lunch breaks and play games of 21 for money. There would be 15 or 18 of us on a good day and we'd put a nickel each in a circle on the ground and start shooting. Not to be a braggart, but I made a lot of extra lunch money because of all the practicing I had done.

Making the school team was another matter entirely. I tried out in the seventh grade and got cut. I tried out in the eighth grade and got cut. I was wondering about my abilities more than I was playing.

In those years, Coffee High School was for students in grades nine through 12, but the freshmen were allowed to compete with other schools at the junior high level. I tried out for the team and, by golly, Coach Ralph Smith kept me around.

I was a pretty good player by then and we had a good team. The highlight of the season was playing in the Spring Valley Invitational Tournament. I made the all-tournament team and that came close to topping my baseball excursion to Cleveland as the thrill of my life.

I can't think of anything negative about my years at Coffee High School. Nor can I imagine there being a better high school to attend. I developed lifelong friendships during those four years and it's always a little emotional going back to that campus.

I want this to be taken in the proper way, not as if I'm bragging. But several years ago when they named the Coffee High School gymnasium in my honor, I was as proud as a full feathered peacock. I'm extremely thankful for that gesture.

Similarly, I'm appreciative of three grand things that happened during my sophomore year of high school. First, I started taking notice of a younger girl named Annette Harrison, who was as popular as she was pretty. Second, I got to play on the junior varsity basketball team and be coached for the first time by Hayden Riley, who has been a champion in my life.

Third, I got my driver's license, by the hardest.

My mother walked to work most days. However, we had a 1940 Ford convertible that had a badly leaking cloth top we kept trying to repair. But try as we did, that thing would gush water every time it rained.

So when the time came for me to go get my driver's license, a guy who rented a room upstairs from Mary Snow said I could use his car for my road test. I washed his car for him all the time, so he was pleased to help out.

Well, that car had a problem, too. Every time you pushed back the seat for leg room, after about five minutes the rear of the seat would spring forward.

As luck would have it, I was doing the parking portion of the road test when the seat sprung forward and almost sent the state trooper through the windshield. I pushed it back and apologized. Then about five minutes later it happened again, this time worse, and the state trooper almost banged his head a second time.

I'll never forget the look on his face and the tone of his voice when he said, "Son, if you're going to get your driver's license, you're going to get this seat fixed."

Coach Riley was a little more encouraging in his dealings with me. After starting my sophomore season on the junior varsity team, he moved me up to the varsity and I got to play some. That was an invaluable experience, a boost in confidence.

But lettering as a sophomore meant I was at the mercy of juniors and seniors when it came to initiation into the C Club. That was a dreadful deal because they did some bad things to you.

So when I got finished with lunch during the initiation period, which seemed to last forever, I went behind the band room and hid because the juniors and seniors were running free during that time and I didn't want to have anything to do with them.

It didn't do any good because they caught up with me, tied an end of rope around my testicles, tied an end of rope around my neck and put a sign on my back that said "ring the bell." Fortunately, I had a sweatshirt I put on when they weren't around. That allowed me minimize an embarrassing situation.

Then on C Club initiation night, the worst of it all, they blindfolded us and put us in the back of a truck. They took us out in the wilderness someplace, made us eat some mess that made our mouths pucker, made us eat a raw oyster with a string attached to it and made us drink some awful concoction that made us throw up. Then they left us out there to find our way home, each of us all alone in an out of the way place.

It was a pretty night, with the moon shining, but I didn't have any idea where we were. I had been peeking a little on the ride out and knew we had gone past a little place called Bar-Bar and it appeared we were in Waterloo or Central.

Well, I took to walking down country roads. I walked and walked and walked — and fretted about never getting back. Finally, I came up on a house and knocked on the door. Well, to my amazement, the man who answered was the basketball coach at Central High School. He recognized me, put me in his car and took me home.

My competitive fire was raging when basketball season rolled around during my junior year of high school. That's why so many of those games are memorable.

We had a fine team and made it to the district tournament semifinals, where we were to play T.M. Rogers, one of the finer teams in that part of the state. In fact, they had already beaten us three times that season.

We made it through regulation and an overtime and the game was still tied. In those days, you played sudden death at that point and that's what happened.

Our plan was to get the basketball to Ray Carpenter, our center. He caught a pass but couldn't get off a shot. So he passed it to me. I threw it up and, swish, it went in for the winning basket.

We were fortunate enough to win the district tournament and advance to the state tournament in Tuscaloosa, which is a major thrill for a high school player.

In our first game at Foster Auditorium on the University of Alabama campus we played Pell City. Bobby Skelton was their star player, he being the former Crimson Tide quarterback and a National Football League official.

We won in the first round and faced Carbon Hill in the second round. Interestingly, that's where I would later start my coaching career. Lloyd Nix, a future Auburn University quarterback, was one of their stars.

The game was scheduled to start at ten o'clock in the morning, the first of the day, and Coach Riley had a brainstorm during the previous night. Since Foster Auditorium only had a scoreboard on one end of the court, he told us we would get to the gym early and start warming up on the other end. That'd enable us to shoot at the basket with the only scoreboard near it during the fourth quarter.

So we got there early, only to find out Carbon Hill had come up with the same strategy and was already on the court loosening up. They beat us in a close game, too, and that might have been my most disappointing day while at Coffee High School.

One of the more embarrassing moments during my high school years came during summer, when I worked at Reynolds Aluminum. There were three shifts, eight to four, four to 12 and 12 to eight, and it was hard labor. I stacked sheets of aluminum, carefully, because if it got scratched you'd catch the devil.

The midnight shift was a time when some people got a little lax and found a place to take short naps. I was warned right off to never do that, told that a worker caught asleep got his shoes painted. I wasn't sure I believed that because I was the guy they picked on a lot, anyway, like the time they sent me to look for striped paint and I didn't catch on to the joke.

Well, one night I was pooped, so I slipped off and found a desk with a stack of aluminum in front of it. It wasn't long before my head was down and I was snoozing. Then came a strong smell that awakened me, wet paint, bright orange, all on my shoes.

Memories of those days and nights at Reynolds Aluminum bring to mind thoughts of the most unusual job I had during my high school years.

Barry Hibbett, a dear friend who has passed away, heard about a summer job that sounded like fun. He asked if I was interested in helping a veterinarian go from store to store in town after town in Lauderdale County vaccinating dogs. I asked him the pay. He said we would get $50 a week, plus lunch every day.

So every dog that came up there yelping and hollering, growling and tugging at chains, Barry and I held while the veterinarian shot them. That was a loud summer, with dogs carrying on all across Lauderdale County.

When we got back to school and people asked about the summer, I told them Barry and I worked shooting dogs. Of course, that prompted some curious looks until I explained the unique opportunity we had.

During my spare time I would go over to Florence State Teachers College to play basketball with a bunch of guys, some of them in high school, like me, and some of them in college. The gym was locked on weekends, but we found a way to push up the girls' bathroom window and get in there. Then after we finished we'd take a skinny dip in a nice and cool pool they had in the building.

It wasn't breaking and entering, I don't guess, because we didn't break anything. However, there wasn't any doubt we could have gotten in a lot of trouble for what we did.

And, of course, there was the afternoon a bunch of administrators showed up unannounced as we were swimming naked in the pool. We were a hustling and bustling beanbag group trying to gather our shorts and get out of there through the girls' bathroom window on that occasion.

My senior year at Coffee High School was fairly uneventful, other than the fact I was elected class president. We didn't make it to the state tournament in basketball, which was a disappointment, but I made it to graduation despite being woefully weak in algebra.

Barry, who had six brothers and is a member of the family that owns Hibbett Sporting Goods, was the vice president of our class. His house was across the street from the high school and that was where we gathered to march toward our commencement, with me in front and my good buddy just behind me.

I noticed Barry had lost the tassel from his cap and quickly said something I regret today: "Oh, Barry, you've lost your tou-sell." Everybody heard dumb me mispronounce tassel as tou-sell and it took several months for the ridicule to cease.

Maybe I was about as bad in English and speech as I was in algebra.

I wasn't great in basketball, either, but good enough to attract the attention of a few colleges. I could shoot, but I was slow.

Joel Eaves, the coach at Auburn, called and said he'd get me a scholarship to Young Harris Junior College and then bring me on board after I polished my skills. I pondered that and decided against it.

That would have been extremely interesting, ol' Wimp down on The Plains, especially considering how I fought tooth and nail with Auburn as an assistant coach and, to a lesser degree, as a head coach.

I had an opportunity to go to Southern Miss for visit and left thinking I had a scholarship. I found out differently just after I returned home.

I thumbed over to Starkville, Mississippi to try out for Coach Babe McCarthy. Obviously, I wasn't good enough to make that outstanding team.

I didn't know what to do. Then one morning at Sunday School,

Barry told me he was going to Abilene Christian University, that he thought I could get a basketball scholarship.

A few weeks later, a football player from Athens, Alabama came by and said he was going to Abilene Christian on a scholarship and he understood they wanted me to come out to Texas on a basketball scholarship.

I talked back and forth with the folks at Abilene Christian and they sent me a partial scholarship in the mail without seeing me play. I've made a few recruiting blunders through the years, but I've never done anything quite like that.

Then came the crushing news. My pal Barry dropped by the apartment one day and said he wasn't going to Abilene Christian, after all. After all that work, I was stuck with the prospect of going to a strange place all alone.

I got on a train with some chicken and a sack of apples and took off for Texas. I didn't eat the first piece of chicken before I realized I was making a terrible mistake. When I got out there and saw nothing more than barbed wire and a lot of wind, my fears were confirmed.

Besides, I was dating Annette and I missed her. She and my mom came for a visit one time during the first semester, which was fun, but it was a long and expensive trip and I knew it wouldn't happen often.

So I was left with a special memory from their visit. When Annette and my mother arrived, all of the boys started hollering, "Hey, Alabama, your girl is here." I raced outside, as excited a child on Christmas Day, and we had such a good time it's more than a little memorable.

To summarize the Texas Abilene experience, I lived in barracks with some genuine cowboys, went to the Oklahoma-Texas football game, went to the Texas State Fair in Dallas and by the end of the first semester decided to go home and enroll at Florence State Teachers College.

Ed Billingham was the coach at Florence State and they didn't give out scholarships of much value. It might have been only $75 per month. Maybe it was that plus tuition.

But I was living at home, back in Florence, and was able to play basketball in my home town for three years.

Charlie Frederick, one of my teammates at Coffee High School was on our team. So was Dabs Earnest, a terrific player who had been in military service and wanted to play basketball after being discharged. Several years later, I was his presenter when he was inducted in the University of North Alabama Hall of Fame. Sadly, he has passed away. Also on that team were Max Burleson, "Jelly Belly" Bush and some others that made it fun.

Coach Billingham was a delightful man and he made me ride shotgun with him when we went to games in a short convoy of cars. Well, that scared me to death because he was color blind and couldn't tell red from green. I was afraid he would run a traffic light and kill everybody in the car.

Max was a great guy and he was driving a Chevrolet right in front of us. So I told Coach Billingham that it appeared Max was smoking in the car ahead of us, that maybe he should get Max in the car with him and let me drive the other car to the game. Coach Billingham fell for it hook, line and sinker and I had a much safer trip.

I wasn't trying to get Max in trouble. I was trying to save my life and get home from that road trip.

We were a pretty ragged basketball team with considerably ragged means. We ate our pregame meals at a bowling alley, a hamburger or some other type sandwich, and we put some milk in the back of the cars to drink after games.

But Coach Billingham insisted we look sharp, wear ties, and I'll never forget the afternoon "Little Red" Thomas, a setshot artist and a great player, showed up without one. He wasn't going to get to eat the pregame meal because of it. So he slipped off to a shoe shop next door to the bowling alley, got a set of shoestrings and made him a little bow tie out of them.

We didn't win much at Florence State, only had between fair and good teams, but I made a lot of good friends and will always be grateful for the opportunity.

The best part, of course, was being able to spend time with Annette. We had started dating in high school when she was a sophomore and I was a senior. We had been going together for a long time, so we decided we'd get married on October 26, 1957, just before the start of another basketball season.

It's interesting that we eventually discovered my dad, who died when I was six, and her dad, who died when she was two, worked together at Campbell Motor Company in Florence. Also, later we learned we went to the same kindergarten, so I guess you could say we've been soul mates most of our lives.

Let me tell you a little more about Annette.

Annette was a special girl, extremely popular in high school. She has so many wonderful characteristics it's easy for people to like her. It doesn't take long for that to happen, either, because she's so personable in a quiet, reserved and polite way.

As for her performance as a wife and the mother of three fine sons, I won't attempt to describe how much I admire her because I'd never find the proper words. She's just terrific, great in all areas, and I'm thankful for all of the things she has done for me.

Read on and those things will become obvious. If nothing else, she deserves a medal for putting up with me on game days and a place in heaven for dealing with me after the ones we lost.

If you haven't noticed, I could get pretty uptight while watching my teams in action.

That was also the case on the day Annette and I got married because of a tuxedo mixup.

Somehow, I ended up with tux pants that had been rented for Annette's brother in law. He was a big guy and I was skinny.

I tried on the pants and they dwarfed me. There wasn't any way to keep them up, not even with suspenders.

Back in those days, you weren't suppose to talk to your bride on your wedding day. It was considered bad luck. But I had to do something, so I telephoned Annette and told her about those drooping pants.

I don't recall exactly how we made the swap, but at some point that day I got the right pants. Then, to my dismay, I found out I had his coat when I started dressing for the wedding. Ultimately, I made another swap with him, getting back my coat, and walked to the alter dressed properly.

After all of the fanfare, I was as calm as a baby sound asleep when Annette and I were married at Jackson Heights Church of Christ in Florence. It just goes to show how there are some things you can be sure about.

We got a little apartment on Wood Avenue in Florence. It was right behind a house Ann and Barry Hibbett lived in, which made it more enjoyable. Also, our place was beside Barbara and Ronnie Smith, a couple of our former classmates, which added to the enjoyment.

The apartment barely had turnaround room, but it was fine for us because we knew it'd be a struggle just to make it. In that regard, Annette worked several jobs. She had one at Laramore Business College, among others, until I got my degree from Florence State in 1959.

It was time for me to get a job, hopefully as a coach, and we had another family member on the way. Jim, our oldest son, was born on August 30, 1959 and the weeks leading up to his arrival were hectic because I was having a hard time getting hired.

The major problem was my lack of experience in football. I hadn't played a lick and, as most people know, that's an important sport in Alabama. High schools needed coaches who knew football. I only knew what one looked like, that it was impossible to dribble one.

So it was looking grim. I went to the Alabama State Coaches Clinic with Bearl Whitsett and pretty much begged for a chance. But nothing worked out. However, while in Tuscaloosa I learned Hollis Thompson, the basketball coach at Carbon Hill High School, was going to leave that position to become the principal.

I got in touch with Hollis and he asked me to come down for an interview. I learned that as basketball coach one of my jobs would be to coach baseball. That was fine. I learned that as basketball coach one of my jobs would be to coach football. That was a major problem.

Adding to the football dilemma was the fact Carbon Hill had won a state championship the year before, with future Crimson Tide standout Cotton Clark starring, and that meant the townspeople wanted a repeat although most of the good players were gone. Brick Mason was the new coach. He was a Southern Miss standout who once scored a bunch of touchdowns in a rare victory over Coach Harold "Red" Drew and his Alabama team.

I assured them I'd do my best to learn some football so I could help the team. Somehow, I got the job as head basketball coach, which was a miracle within itself, and as assistant football coach, which was more unbelievable.

To make a long story short, we didn't win a football game that season. I felt somewhat responsible because they'd send me to scout the next opponent when I didn't know the difference in a Single Wing and a Notre Dame Box. Ultimately, they put me with the junior high school team to develop young players.

Do you know what we did most of the time?

We practiced recovering fumbles. I'd line them up and make them knock the dog out of each other while recovering fumbles. That's all I contributed. I never did check the Carbon Hill stats for future games when those young players were in action to see how many fumbles they caused and how many fumbles they recovered. They should have been darn good at it.

Another problem I had was teaching. I had freshman science, Alabama history, civics and physical education. After the first semester, they added senior democracy.

I was in a foreign environment in the classroom. Remember, I couldn't even pronounce tassel until I had been ridiculed into learning how.

As an example of my ineptness, consider the way I taught Alabama history. I'd let each student read a paragraph out of the textbook. We'd keep going like that the entire hour. But when we got to all those rivers, towns and counties with Indian names and I knew I couldn't pronounce them, I'd just say, "Skip it and move to the next page."

By comparison, we had a really outstanding basketball team, which means I got off to a fast start in the profession I desired.

We had Frank Nix, who later attended Alabama and got close to the athletics department. He died several years ago after being a tremendous supporter of University of Alabama basketball while I was there. I'm appreciative of that, plus the way he played for Carbon Hill High School.

We had Dwight Norris, who was a fine player who continued his career at Walker Junior College in Jasper, Alabama and at Austin Peay.

Doug Key played for us. He has coached at the high school level in Alabama for a number of years.

Those were our leaders, but I'll never forget all of the others who played that year, like Buford Edgle and Merlin Guthrie. That group produced a 25-4 record, which should tell you how good they were and how pleased I was to get off to that kind of start.

It was a grand experience and there are a lot of stories people still tell about my first year as a coach.

One involves the old gym at Carbon Hill High School. It was nothing like the first coming of Madison Square Garden in New

York or The Boston Garden. It was a cramped place as cold as a rock during winter. So Billy McDonald, my manager who years later became Alabama's trainer, had to start the fire in the gas generator before we could start practice or play games.

Another story involves the pregame meals my players ate. They were nothing like the elaborate steaks they eat today, simply put, eggs and bacon in our little apartment — and only before rivals were to be played.

Two good memories, or painful ones, involved Herman Cook, a junior that year, who smoked cigarettes. They point out how tough I was on players early in my career, as well as how much I needed to learn.

I was riding back to Carbon Hill from Jasper after a game and came up beside a car and caught Herman smoking. To say I ran him until he fell out on the floor is an understatement. I made the other guys pick him up and made him run some more.

That was foolish on my part, but I was young and didn't know any better.

Then I caught Herman with a cigarette again with other students in what was called the bull ring, a designated smoking area. I let him have it again.

Then Herman sprained an ankle and I thought we needed him for a game. I should have known how to take care of an injury like that, but for some reason I thought intense heat as quickly as possible was the cure.

I filled up a bucket and put his ankle in scalding hot water. Every time Herman tried to pull it out, I jammed it back in. Finally, the ankle swelled so much you could barely recognize he had a foot. My stupidity almost left him without an ankle.

Frank and Dwight used to get a lot of mileage out of a story about me getting fired up for a game against Russellville. That was natural because Russellville had been a major rival when I played at Coffee High School and I wanted my players at

Carbon Hill to feel the same way.

Well, we went on the court against Russellville and played simply great. During the first half, we were shooting the lights out and got in their faces on defense. We went to the dressing room that night leading by 12 or 15 points.

I know my players expected me to brag on them and tell them how proud I was with the way they had played. But I ate their lunch, really got on them about anything I could find wrong with their first half performance.

Then I left them alone to think about how bad they were. At that point, I'm told, Dwight punched Frank and said, "Was I looking at that scoreboard correctly? I thought we were ahead."

Believe me, Carbon Hill was an interesting place to live.

The first time Annette went downtown to buy groceries, she came up on a man in the back of a truck with a sheet over him. Somebody had shot him.

We lived behind the school in a downstairs apartment. I remember coming in one night and finding a safe in the road leading to our house. It seems somebody had robbed the school late that afternoon.

I had an evening to remember that year, too, because that was a rugged area of Walker County where there were a bunch of bootleggers and other type characters. Frank Nix's daddy was Brunner Nix, the sheriff, which was an awesome responsibility during that time.

One evening we were at the Nix's house having dinner. In fact, it was the night before the election and Brunner said, "Coach Sanderson, I've got to go out to some mine shafts and check on some people who are reportedly exchanging whiskey for votes. Would you like to go with me?"

Now, if I'm not the biggest coward in the nation, I'm at least in the top five. But I said, "Sure, I'll go with you."

It was spooky up in that area and it was misting rain. I was looking left and right for shady characters, rustlers and the like, particularly anybody with a gun. Well, I had my head turned and was looking to the right, playing deputy, when Brunner turned on the windshield wipers. I jumped out of my skin when I heard those wipers getting started. I thought I had been shot.

When I first took the job at Carbon Hill, Annette and Jim were still in Florence because he was too young to make the trip. So I moved into the apartment without them and took in Hosea Collins, a friend from Florence State who was an assistant football coach. He stayed with me until my family could get there, which meant the place was always a mess.

To say Jim, Annette and Wimp Sanderson didn't have much is the understatement of the year. We skirted orange crates, which is where I kept my underwear and socks and she kept her clothes. We took a huge cable spool, put a cloth over it and used it as a bedside table.

I bought a refrigerator for five dollars and a stove for five dollars. Also, we bought a cheap living room suit. Other than our beds, that was the extent of our household furnishings.

The refrigerator was a major problem because it froze everything in sight — eggs, milk, oranges, you name it.

Then there was the night I stumbled to that refrigerator in search of a baby bottle for Jim. It was my night to feed him and I was tired and draggy. I opened the refrigerator, grabbed the bottle, put water in the pan and put the pan on the stove. Then I went into the living room, sat down and took a quick nap while waiting for the water to get hot enough to warm the bottle. Then I put in the bottle.

Well, a few minutes later I went into the kitchen to check on the milk and discovered I was heating a bottle of ketchup.

Now you know I had a lot to learn as a new father and a lot to learn as a new coach.

Actually, we won our first seven games, then went to Dora to play the next one. We got down 52-38 to the Bulldogs, so I decided it was time to take a timeout and go to a pressing defense. Miraculously, we came back to tie the score, but lost a close one.

I didn't sleep for three days. I'd lay there and worry, worry, worry and worry some more.

Believe me when I say that carried over to other places, particularly the University of Alabama. I just never could seem to get over losses. All of them hurt me to no end, but the bigger the stakes, the bigger the anguish.

Tournament time was murder because it was one loss and adios, at the high school level and the college level.

We had a bad draw in the district tournament that first year and ended up playing a fine Tuscaloosa County High School team coached by Adrian McKenzie, one of the greats in state sports history. He had Buster Sullivan on his team, a future University of Alabama player, and Clark Boler, another good one. They beat us and went on to win the state championship.

We packed up the equipment, went back to Carbon Hill and started getting ready for the next season.

But next year never came for me in Carbon Hill because I got the break of a lifetime.

I went down to the state tournament, ran into Coach Hayden Riley, who was an assistant coach on the University of Alabama basketball staff, and was more than a little interested when he told me Coach Eugene Lambert might be about to resign from the Crimson Tide program. He told me he might want me to come to Tuscaloosa and help him if he was named head coach.

The plan Coach Riley outlined was for me to work with the freshman team while working on my Master's Degree. That sounded good, really exciting, and I was on Cloud Nine when I got back to Carbon Hill.

Time passed and I dropped Coach Riley a note and told him I'd like to try what he suggested if the opportunity came along. Of course, I didn't expect it to happen.

But one day I was on the way to baseball practice at Carbon Hill High School and heard on the radio that Dr. Lambert had resigned and was going to return to Memphis State as an athletics department administrator.

After a little trying, I hooked up with Coach Riley and he asked me to come down for a visit.

That was the first time I met Coach Paul "Bear" Bryant, who would become a major influence. I was visiting with Coach Riley in the lobby and he introduced us.

Coach Bryant thought the world of Coach Riley, who had helped with football recruiting and other matters in addition to being an assistant basketball coach. I knew Coach Bryant respected what he thought, so I felt pretty good.

I learned on that trip Leif Carlson, a former Michigan State player under John Bennington and Pete Newell, planned to stay on the coaching staff. Also, I learned the job I was talking about taking wouldn't pay much and Annette would be our principal bread winner again.

Eventually, I became the graduate assistant basketball coach at the University of Alabama, as Coach Riley had outlined, and the Sanderson family was ready to embark on a new adventure.

As I told you we didn't own much, but what we did have had to go with us. So we decided to rent an old coal truck for the move.

When we started loading up, we got the refrigerator with a big round top to the door and watched it get away from us. It rolled all the way to the bottom of the hill leading to the house. Rather than mess with it, I left it there for somebody to have — all $5 worth.

We loaded the coal truck to the hilt and wrapped rope underneath it and over everything we had piled on top.

At that time I owned a 1955 black Studebaker car, a President, a real doozie. Annette, Jim and I sent the driver of the coal truck ahead, stayed around for a while to take care of a few other matters and started rolling toward Tuscaloosa.

We figured we'd pass the coal truck along the way, but we never saw the darn thing. Nor did we see it when we arrived in Tuscaloosa. Finally, it came rolling in and everything we owned was barely hanging on the back. I never have figured out where that guy made a wrong turn, but I definitely assumed he did.

We started unloading at Bakersfield Apartments, a complex the University of Alabama owned and rented. Not only was our apartment small, it was made out of cardboard and was hot in the summer and cold in the winter. There wasn't an in between season at that place.

But it was cheap, no more than $35 per month, utilities included, and it was a roof over our heads.

Still, it was a hot roof when we moved in and since I had recently bought an air conditioning unit in Carbon Hill, I decided without much coaxing that I had to get it installed. Tuscaloosa was blazing and unbelievably humid, as it always is during summer, and it was so uncomfortable Jim couldn't sleep at night.

Now I'm not much of a fix-it-up person, not by any stretch, but after about five hours I had that air conditioner in place and was excited about turning it on. But when I started plugging it in, nothing happened because it was a 220-volt unit and the apartment was wired for 110.

I put an ad in the newspaper faster than you can hiccup, sold the 220, bought a 110 and, thank goodness, got that thing running before we suffocated.

The old Studebaker was coming undone, too, and I went to see my friend Howard Killen, who owned the Dodge place in Florence. I went up there to buy some tires for it. But while I was on his lot, he talked me into buying a station wagon.

Oh, what a stupid mistake that was. It was expensive. It had the worst brakes you've ever seen. It was like driving a hearse.

The bad part was showing up at Bakersfield Apartments in a new Dodge station wagon. Much later, after they got to know us better, several of the students living there told me they thought I was a rich basketball coach after seeing me roll into the complex in that new car.

Little did those students know.

Not only had we stepped down a notch or a few when it came to housing, we had been at a woefully low level in Carbon Hill.

We got a break the following year, 1961, after long enough in Bakersfield Apartments. Gene "Bebes" Stallings, then an assistant coach on Coach Bryant's football staff, and his wife, Ruth Ann, moved out of a house they rented in Abrams Place. By a stroke of luck, we were able to rent it.

As I recall, the rent for that two-bedroom house was $65 per month. It was a steal, even for a family living with modest means, and we stayed there seven years.

To give you a little more idea of how poor we were at that time, we moved to Abrams Place in a pickup truck — and I rode to our new house while sitting in a platform rocker among all the furniture in the back. I recall having to get down as low as I could in the bed when a police car appeared.

I can't remember everything I was thinking about making such a dramatic change, a fast move from coaching at the high school level to coaching at the collegiate level.

I'm sure I was apprehensive about accepting the task of coaching college players who weren't that much younger than me because I had done the same thing to a lesser extent with high school players.

On the flip side, I loved the idea of being associated with a basketball program that competed in the Southeastern Conference. There weren't many like that, I reasoned, and Alabama was one of a few with a proud tradition. Also, I knew Hayden Riley, my high school coach, would do all he could to keep me from falling flat on my face.

So the treacherous trip from West Tuscaloosa Street to

Tuscaloosa ended happily enough. I was living in a house for the first time in my life and my family was putting down deep roots.

At last, we were in a city we could call home. We were there 32 years, long enough to build super friendships, a reputation for winning and memories that will last a lifetime.

Still, it wasn't long enough.

CHAPTER TWO

He Will Always Be Coach Bryant to Me

*Wimp Sanderson was a fiery young assistant coach
under Hayden Riley at the University of Alabama*

After arriving in Tuscaloosa to start work as a graduate assistant coach on the basketball staff it didn't take long for me to figure out who was totally in charge of the University of Alabama Athletics Department. In fact, I watched in utter disbelief as Paul "Bear" Bryant, the great football coach, cast what could be termed a magical spell over everybody.

That was in 1960, as the Crimson Tide football program shook off the last of the negative effects of a terrible run through the middle part of the 1950s and appeared on the verge of regaining national prominence. The program had experienced victory only four times from 1954 through 1957 under embattled Coach J.B. "Ears" Whitworth, so the 5-4-1, 7-2-1 and 8-1-2 records Coach Bryant produced in 1958, 1959 and 1960 rekindled what had been dampened spirits.

As I've stated, I didn't know much about football at the time, but I could recognize excitement when I saw it. I could see why Alabama was successful. Also, the enthusiasm for football sort of spilled over into the entire athletics department, which helped those of us laboring in other sports.

Right up front let me tell you I don't consider myself one of Coach Bryant's boys. I didn't play football for him, nor for anybody, for that matter. But I was fortunate enough to develop what I'd term a wonderful relationship with him and I'm appreciative of that and all of the things he did to help me.

You won't hear me refer to him in any way other than Coach Bryant, not The Bear or anything like that, because that would be disrespectful to a man I admired.

I don't think I've ever seen anybody quite like Coach Bryant. He was a tireless worker, a fearless competitor and, more than anything, a gifted leader. I don't think it's fair to him to make the comparison, but I couldn't help but learn something about how to run a program while watching him in those early years.

Coach Bryant was an excellent athletics director. Also, I should said we had a couple of fine ones after him. In fact, Ray Perkins and Steve Sloan impressed me in a significant way. I'll tell you much more about those at times misunderstood men in a later chapter when I talk about an athletics department that had some ups and downs.

For now, let's get back to Coach Bryant, who had a presence about him nobody else ever had, unless it was a military leader or a gifted evangelist. Everybody seemed to rally around him, wait for his commands, and If he walked into a room unannounced, everybody got quiet and waited to hear what he had to say. It was a deportment I can't adequately explain.

I can say Coach Bryant was a tremendous handler of people, his players and his staff, and everybody knows he was one of the foremost football coaches in history, if not the best.

Several examples of how Coach Bryant handled people in such a skillful manner come to mind easily. But the best might be how he dealt with me just after my appointment as head basketball coach in 1980.

I was the happiest man in the world that day. I was honored because Coach Bryant and Coach Sam Bailey, his chief assistant athletics director, had considered numerous options and had decided I was the man for the job. C.M. Newton played a role in my appointment, too, because he recommended me.

I've heard Coach Bryant thought I was a hard worker and was loyal to the program and wanted to give me a chance to prove myself as a head coach. Other than that, I don't know what he thought about me.

A few days after Coach Bailey introduced me as the new coach at a press conference, I went to thank Coach Bryant for the opportunity the school had given me. I knocked on his office door and he opened it.

I told him how appreciative I was and thanked him for the confidence he had displayed.

He said, "I didn't have a damn thing to do with it."

When he paused, I struggled for something to say. I was nervous. Thank goodness, he got me off the hook when he said, "But I damn sure could have stopped it."

I told him I understand that and that's why I was there, to thank him personally. I didn't tell him I planned to emulate much that he had done because of the success he had.

People have asked me how Coach Bryant won so much. His secret, I'm convinced, at least one of many, was how he organized a coaching staff. When he arrived at Alabama in 1958 from Texas A&M, he put together the finest assortment of assistant coaches I've ever seen. On that staff he had Gene "Bebes" Stallings, who isn't a stranger to Crimson Tide fans, John David Crow, his Heisman Trophy winner from Texas A&M, Jerry Claiborne, Howard Schnellenberger, Pat James and Dude Hennessey, all former players from his years at Kentucky, and others who knew football strategy better than most head coaches.

As I think about the respect Coach Bryant commanded, it reminds me of a humorous story that involved a janitorial worker we all loved to be around. His name was Chester Hicks, who liked to tell a joke or two. All of the assistant coaches on the football staff would meet him every morning in a rear room at the old athletics department building on University Boulevard. There were several times when I'd join them.

I can't count the mornings Chester would be in the middle of a colorful story or be near the punch line of a joke only to have Coach Bryant appear in the room. Then the same thing happened. He'd grab a dust cloth or a broom and started cleaning everything in sight, whether it needed it or not. We missed a lot of good stories because the football coach and athletics director showed up at a bad time.

Also, that meant all of those assistant football coaches had to hurry to work, which produced wonders because in 1961 Alabama was an unbeaten and untied national champion.

For what it's worth, our basketball team the first season I was on campus had a 7-18 record, worst in the Southeastern Conference, and we followed that the next season with an 11-15 record. The year after that we improved drastically, to 14-11, a winner at last.

But it doesn't take a math wizard to determine we were no match for the football program, which played less than half as many games and won almost as many as we did.

Fortunately for me, I was impressed by what football was accomplishing, which brings to mind one of my favorite memories from those early years. It deals with the arrival of quarterback Joe Namath on campus while he was being recruited by Howard Schnellenberger. As most people in our part of the nation know, he was a standout from Beaver Falls, Pennsylvania who had originally committed to play at Maryland. He struggled with the entrance exams and couldn't get in that school.

I was in a back room at the athletics department when Howard appeared with Joe during the spring of 1961. They were going to football practice. Joe had on a plaid sport coat and a straw hat and he had a toothpick in his mouth. I said to myself, "Who in the world is this character?" About a quarter of an hour later, Joe became one of only a few people who were allowed to stand on top of the observation tower Coach Bryant used during practices. When that word got out, the media wrote about it, wrote about it and wrote about it some more.

The recruitment worked and the University of Alabama had one of its most famous players in the fold.

I was fortunate to be around two great Crimson Tide

quarterbacks, Joe Namath and Kenny Stabler, because I taught a physical education class. I remember how scared I was one of them would get hurt and I'd have to tell Coach Bryant. Those fears were unfounded, thank goodness, and both or them got an "A" grade in my class.

Now that I've talked gloriously about Alabama football, which I followed with enthusiasm, let me talk a little about the position Crimson Tide basketball had during those years, particularly as it relates to Coach Bryant.

A lot has been said about Coach Bryant leaving Kentucky after the 1953 football season because he couldn't stand playing second fiddle to Coach Adolph Rupp and the basketball program. The story goes they gave Coach Rupp a Cadillac after he won the Southeastern Conference championship and they gave Coach Bryant a watch.

Everybody associated with the Alabama basketball program knew about that story and I guess there was a concern that Coach Bryant really didn't care about our sport.

That might have been true during my early years on campus, when we played in old and cramped Foster Auditorium. Basketball was sort of like a stepchild as Coach Bryant went about the business of restoring the football program. There just wasn't much interest in what we were doing, at least not that I could tell.

I found out I was wrong several years later, like in February of 1968, when we moved out of Foster Auditorium into new and spacious Memorial Coliseum. The pecking order remained intact, with basketball lagging behind football in importance, but Coach Bryant began showing a fresh interest in our sport. I think he realized a lot of money could be made for the athletics department because the arena seated 15,043, basketball was starting to secure some pleasing television contracts and the popularity of the sport was on the rise.

It was not as if we were faltering altogether, because Coach

Hayden Riley recorded some grand wins during his tenure. Maybe the highlights were back-to-back victories over Tennessee and Kentucky at Foster Auditorium, home sweeps of prestigious programs. We whipped the Vols there in 1964 and 1965, 67-64 and 63-58, and we whipped the Wildcats there those same seasons, 65-59 and 75-71. That was a load, for sure, because they were considered national powers, and I think it says a lot about the type coach Hayden Riley was and could have been in a better situation.

But a lot was going on then, like an impending coaching change. Coach Riley, my mentor and dear friend until his death, had a 102-104 record from 1961 through 1968, with me contributing as an assistant coach, and Coach Bryant decided to make a change. He hired C.M. Newton, an obscure choice who had been at Transylvania College in Lexington, Kentucky.

Maybe that coaching change was another reason for the stronger and more visible interest Coach Bryant had in basketball. I do know C.M. didn't have to help with football recruiting like Hayden had during his many years of service, which meant he could focus only on our sport.

But as much as Coach Bryant seemed to change during the late 1960s, he did have some interest in basketball during the early part of that decade, particularly when Kentucky came to town to play Alabama in Foster Auditorium. I think he had a genuine respect for that basketball program.

Every year when that game came around, Bert Bank, a local businessman, would have Coach Rupp as a dinner guest at his house. He would have Coach Bryant over, too, because they had known each other while working together in Lexington from 1946 through 1953. A few of us underlings got to tag along.

I never have figured out what the relationship was between the two famous coaches at that time. I think they were friends. At the least they were cordial toward each other.

One night we were on the lake at Bert Bank's place. Coach

Rupp, who enjoyed bourbon, had a few strong snorts and seemed to be having fun.

When we left the dinner party, Sam Bailey was driving the car, Coach Riley was in the front seat and I was in the back seat with Coach Rupp. I was just a whippersnapper who was glad to be there, a young coach sitting beside possibly the most famous basketball coach in history.

Then, lo and behold, Coach Rupp keeled over and his head fell squarely in my lap. I didn't know what to do. I was frightened. I didn't know if Coach Rupp had gone to sleep, passed out from too much alcohol or was dead.

I was helpless. I started to say something to Coach Riley and Coach Bailey, then decided against it. Finally, I grabbed Coach Rupp by the shoulders and gave him a gentle nudge. In a snap, his head came up, he repositioned himself in the seat and nothing was ever said.

I can't tell you how relieved I was just to see his eyes open.

Also, it meant a lot to me when Coach Bryant came to basketball games. That didn't happen that often during the 1960s, for several reasons. He was busy, consumed by football. He couldn't go out in public much because people bothered him. And, as I learned later, like me, he didn't like referees.

We were all proud during the spring of 1973 when Coach Bryant agreed to accompany us to New York City for the National Invitation Tournament. C.M. invited him, asked him to sit on the bench with the team, and he accepted the offer.

We played Manhattan in the opening round and in the heat of a battle at Madison Square Garden Coach Bryant got upset with the officials. Now, be sure, he didn't know if the officiating was good or bad, but he didn't like what he was seeing because some of the calls were hurting us.

We beat Manhattan, 87-86, in an important game in Alabama basketball history. Glenn Garrett made a heave of a shot at the buzzer for the final margin. When we got in the dressing room after it was over, Coach Bryant told C.M. he had gotten so upset with the officials that he almost said something that would have definitely gotten us a penalty.

Coach Newton explained that it isn't a penalty you get in basketball, rather a technical foul, and Coach Bryant got a kick out of that.

In our next game we played Minnesota, which had future New York Yankees baseball star Dave Winfield as its best player. We fell behind 13 points at the half and decided to let Wendell Hudson guard Winfield in the second half. It worked like a charm and we came back to win, 69-65, in another exciting game.

As our players, coaches, managers and trainers danced on the court, a wild celebration, I saw Coach Bryant out there with us. He was doing a jig, too, as thrilled as the rest of us.

Coach Bryant also traveled with our Alabama basketball team when we played Indiana in the NCAA Mideast Regional Tournament during the spring of 1976 in Baton Rouge, Louisiana. That was a classic game. They were unbeaten, the last team to accomplish that, and we might have had Bobby Knight's Hoosiers beat, in my estimation, until a turnover late in the game let them off the hook. They won, 74-69, because it turned into a free throw display in the final minute.

That game started unraveling when one of our stars, Leon Douglas, had an open court collision with one of their stars, Kent Benson. The official called a foul Leon. That wasn't the case, or at least it appeared that way from vantage point. It was a crucial call that might have cost our team a great victory. In fact, Coach Knight said after that season that had his team not won the national championship, Alabama probably would have.

Take that for what it's worth, which is a bunch as far as I'm concerned because it shows how one call can hurt. In that case it could have cost us a national championship because that was a heck of a basketball team.

Looking three years back, without question, that was an ingenious move on C.M.'s part inviting Coach Bryant to go to New York for the NIT. His presence on our bench certainly seemed to help us. But more importantly he discovered Alabama basketball was moving in the right direction, which added to his enthusiasm. We learned he genuinely cared about Alabama sports as a whole and liked to see teams from our program have success.

The latter point tells you what an athletics director should be. Coach Bryant was a great one, with a strong assist from Sam Bailey. He was extremely wise, more so than a lot of people who considered him just a great football coach will ever realize, and he had enormous energy.

In fact, Coach Bryant worked hard to help our basketball program. We realized the clout he had with high school prospects, particularly those from our state, and he was more than willing to telephone some of them for us.

That brings to mind our recruitment in the 1960s of George Harrison, a 6-foot-10 center from Sidney Lanier High School in Montgomery. He had a lot of potential, so I went to see Coach Bryant and told him he was coming to campus that weekend for an important visit.

We were constructing Memorial Coliseum at the time and Coach Bryant agreed to go over there with George and me. To this day I've got pictures of Coach Bryant, a tall and skinny high school senior and me walking around that place wearing hardhats.

It was experiences like that, plus a zillion more, that led to me respecting Coach Bryant in a major way. That was the norm among all of us who worked under him. He was unpredictable, no doubt, but always willing to help other coaches.

Dude Hennessey, the longtime Alabama staff member, had that type respect for his former coach, too, and he had a million stories about the man that he enjoyed telling and I enjoyed hearing. Come to think of it, I still love those tales.

Dude likes to talk about how Coach Bryant kept his assistant football coaches under control by setting them up during staff meetings. He'd ask one of them a question, digest the answer and then tear him apart because of what he said. It got to be a running joke with Dude, who kept tabs on who took a verbal lashing and why. It was amusing hearing about those encounters.

Incredulously, Dude said there were times when Coach Bryant wouldn't tell his assistant coaches when staff meetings were scheduled. He made it their responsibility to check with his secretary and find out. Dude said they came at all hours, too, with five o'clock in the morning not an uncommon time.

Dude knew Coach Bryant as well as anybody, having played for him at Kentucky and coached under him, so he became a secretary of sorts for the football staff. If Coach Bryant was out of town, it was his responsibility to know where he was at all times so he wouldn't show up at the athletics department unexpectedly and surprise the assistant coaches.

They all had enormous respect for Coach Bryant. Some might have feared him. Nobody wanted to fail him — and I felt the same way because as our athletics director he was my boss, too.

Although he was as tough as nails, Coach Bryant was terrified of flying unless the weather was good. He wanted to make sure the weight was right, there were two engines and there were two pilots. You get the picture.

Dude said a group consisting of several coaches from Alabama was going to Texas for an event in which Gene Stallings was going to be honored. This was during the late 1970s. There was an assistant coach on the Crimson Tide football staff named Bryant "Tex" Poole, who had relatives out there. He wanted to catch a ride with the coaches going to the event so could spend some time with his kinfolks.

"Tex" walked in Coach Bryant's office and found him working on his yellow legal pad, as was the norm, with his eyeglasses down on his nose. He asked if it would be okay for him to catch a ride on the plane. Without looking up, Coach Bryant said, "Hell, boy, you must weigh 400 pounds."

In reality "Tex" weighed about 250, I'd guess, and I've heard he didn't bother showing up at the airport when the plane was scheduled to leave. I did hear, however, he went on a diet after that and lost about 50 pounds.

But that's the way it was at times with Coach Bryant. He'd say something that'd leave you confused. You thought you knew what he meant, but you could never be sure. He left you dangling and made you think about what he had said.

Steve Sloan, the former Alabama quarterback and athletics director, told me about a time when he called Coach Bryant for some advice. As I recall he was trying to figure out if he should take the job as football coach at Ole Miss.

Steve said by the time the conversation had ended, he thought Coach Bryant had told him to take the job and he thought Coach Bryant had told him not to take the job. What he probably did was give Steve some important things to think about so he could make his own decision.

In that regard, Coach Bryant was a philosopher who had sound ideas about many things and a plan for all occasions. That included his contact with members of the Alabama alumni. He had his close friends, a tiny clique, and he was careful not to get too near to others.

Coach Bryant felt it's important to keep your distance from people who are always wanting to do something for you. He said the more some supporters gave to the program, the more they would want from a coach in return, such as more tickets to games. He said it was imperative to draw the line somewhere.

So it didn't matter if he was counseling somebody or motivating somebody, Coach Bryant was a man who always thought hard before speaking. He knew what he should say before he opened his mouth.

That leads to probably the most important part of his personality, as I viewed it. Coach Bryant wouldn't lie to you. Once he said something, you could take it as what he perceived to be the truth. I always appreciated that and I'm sure others did.

Coach Bryant was even better handling his players, as I discovered on frequent trips to football practice. I loved being out there because I learned something every time I went to watch him at work. He was a great motivator, even during practice. I found out more about his abilities when he invited me to accompany the team for a game against Florida in Gainesville, Florida.

The year was 1979, his last national championship season, and on a hot and humid day his team clobbered a Florida team coached by Charley Pell, 40-0, in an awesome show of power.

Not only was Coach Bryant a great football coach, he had a fantastic wife, Mary Harmon Bryant, and she loved basketball. She'd go to most of our home games, sometimes bringing along Coach Bryant. She told me once how she would make Coach Bryant change seats with her if we started playing bad. Then she told me about games she listened to on the radio while at home.

She said, "Coach Sanderson, you all played good when I was in the kitchen listening and not so good when I was in the living room. It isn't easy having to spend so much time in the kitchen trying to help you win."

Mrs. Bryant said she made Coach Bryant change rooms, too, when they listened to games at home.

Superstitious or not, one season Mrs. Bryant was selected Crimson Tide basketball fan of the year by The Tuscaloosa TipOff Club. She was thrilled by that honor and I was proud, too.

Also, Mrs. Bryant was extremely nice to my wife Annette and me and we counted her among our friends. In fact, after Coach Bryant died we went to visit at her house and were surprised when she asked us to sign some living will papers that said she didn't want to live if she had to be placed on a machine to keep her alive. We signed them because she asked us to.

It's humorous and poignant as I look back and think of some of the things Mrs. Bryant gave me after Coach Bryant died. She gave me some of his golf shoes, some of his sweaters and, to my dismay, some of his pajamas. I've still got a lot of those things, even the pajamas that had little burn holes in them from when he smoked unfiltered Chesterfield cigarettes.

I think Coach Bryant appreciated the hard work C.M. Newton put into refocusing the Alabama basketball program and the hard work the entire staff put into the job. If he had lived long enough, I know he would have been delighted with how far we took the program between 1981 and 1992.

I still laugh when thinking about the day Coach Bryant saw me ambling down the hallway at the athletics department with my shoulders stooped, my head down and my mind churning. It might've been during my first season. It could've been during the second. He caught up with me and said, "Boy, if you don't stop that worrying you're going to drive yourself nuts."

Then there was the time Coach Bryant did drive my friend Jim Bates over the edge. They were going to Greenetrack, near Eutaw, Alabama, to bet on greyhounds. Specifically, they were going after the Big Q playoff.

Jim knew a lot about the dogs and Coach Bryant always wanted to utilize his expertise. So when they got to the track, Jim told him the best bet in the Big Q race was Number 2.

Coach Bryant told him, "No, Jim, I'm going with Number 8."

Jim tried to talk him out of it.

Coach Bryant explained he had seen a car tag with three 8s on it as they were driving to the track, that Number 8 was his dog.

Jim argued with him and won the dispute.

The money went down on Number 2.

Well, the race started and, as Jim expected, Number 8 was in the back of the pack. But they had a big wreck up front, with dogs flying everywhere, and Number 8 got through the mess and went on to win.

Jim said he has never seen a bettor as mad as Coach Bryant was after that race.

Obviously, there are a lot of happy stories about Coach Bryant floating around, even to this day. He touched so many people in a positive manner.

As most people remember, Coach Bryant died on January 26, 1983, a little more than a month after he led Alabama in a football game the last time. I don't remember the exact date, but I can remember the setting in which I saw him the last time. This was after he had announced his retirement and his plans to stay as athletics director until July 1, 1983.

It was a Sunday afternoon and I was in my office studying some film getting ready for a Monday night game against LSU. I went out into the hall to get a swallow or two of water and saw Coach Bryant walking down the hall toward me. He walked into my office and sat on the couch. Naturally, I got a chair and sat down in front of him.

Then he started talking about a multitude of things. He mentioned he probably mishandled Kenny Stabler, The Snake, one of his great Crimson Tide quarterbacks. He talked about the University of Georgia a lot, some problems he thought Coach Vince Dooley and his people might be having. He talked about things he would do differently if he had a second chance. He went on and on with story after story. Then he went to his office.

If I had known that was going to be the last time I would see Coach Bryant, I would've taped that conversation and begged him to keep talking.

On the following Tuesday afternoon, I was practicing my team in preparation for a game at UCLA. Somebody told me Coach

Bryant was in Druid City Hospital, that he had experienced some sharp chest pains the evening before while visiting his dear friend Jimmy Hinton at his house. I was told it didn't look good.

The next afternoon, as we were practicing, somebody told me Coach Bryant had passed away. It was an absolutely sad moment in my life, totally crushing news, and a sorrowful moment for the University of Alabama. I had the added burden of calling together our players and telling them.

His death came at about the time we were to go to Pauley Pavilion in Los Angeles to play UCLA, which was the Number 1 team in the country. In fact, we were scheduled to make that trip the following day, on Thursday morning, for a nationally televised game on Friday night.

I went to talk to Paul Bryant Jr. and Mrs. Bryant and asked if they thought we should cancel the game. Paul Jr. said, "Wimp, I think Papa would want you to go ahead and play." We got some people to sew black patches on our uniforms in his honor.

The funeral was on Friday morning and while we were out in Los Angeles we watched some of the processional that traveled from First United Methodist Church in Tuscaloosa to Elmwood Cemetery in Birmingham. Needless to say, that was an emotional time for me and for everybody else in the travel party.

Our players, being college kids, were moved by what had happened and they were determined to play at their best. Interestingly, we had already won two games in Los Angeles that season, beating Southern Cal and Georgetown in the Winston Tire Classic in December.

When we got to Pauley Pavilion to play UCLA, Coach Terry Donahue, their football coach, was there to greet us. Before the game, he offered a prayer and eulogy in honor of Coach Bryant.

We played a tremendous game, got a good lead and won by two points when Mike Davis, one of our guards, made two clutch free throws. Because of the circumstances, I was as proud of that team that weekend as any I coached. It was a highly charged setting, to say the least, and that game was memorable, if not one of the top ten victories in Alabama basketball history.

But nobody from Alabama felt like a winner the day Coach Bryant died. Nor on the afternoon he was buried. He meant far too much to what seems like a million people, including his basketball coach.

CHAPTER THREE

Eight Tough Years: 1960-1968

Wimp Sanderson, left, and C.M. Newton, right, spent a season coaching together under Coach Hayden Riley at the University of Alabama

I can't start telling you about the turbulent and tough 1960s in University of Alabama basketball without beginning with perhaps the funniest moment Annette and I have had as a wife and a husband. It occurred after we moved from the house we were renting at Abrams Place in Tuscaloosa, Alabama to a great little red brick house on 15th Street.

We got the chance to do that through a strange twist of good fortune that started when Coach Paul "Bear" Bryant hired "Smokey" Harper, his trainer at Texas A&M, to take care of film and to perform other administrative duties for the Alabama football program.

Eventually, "Smokey" and Marie decided they wanted to sell a small but pretty house on 15th Street. Annette and I wanted it, but we had a problem. We didn't have any money, not a spare dime, because I wasn't making peanuts as the lowest coach on the totem pole.

Then we got a break. Coach Bryant or somebody in the Alabama sports information department said I could sell advertising for the programs people bought at football games. They said I could make $1,000 or $1,500 cold cash by going out and renewing contracts with the current advertisers. That sounded like a million bucks to us at that time, so I went out that summer and picked up about $1,200.

We put that money down on the great little red brick house on 15th Street. It had three bedrooms and is where our sons, Jim, Scott and Barry, starting growing up.

What I loved about that house was the yard. It had beautiful zoysia grass, like something you'd see on a golf course, and ample space for the boys to play.

I guess the reason I was so crazy about the yard was because I didn't have one as a child since my mother and I were in an apartment.

Anyway, I had a problem. I loved the yard, but I didn't know diddle about taking care of one. I had mowed my aunt and uncle's yard while growing up in Florence, but when it came to things like fertilizing and weed control, I was beyond the fence in left field.

But that zoysia grass was fantastic and I wanted to keep it that way. So when it came time to fertilize it, I borrowed one of those fancy spreaders from Bill Wood and dumped a huge bag in it.

I started spreading fertilizer and it didn't look like much was coming out, just a few dribbles at a time. So I adjusted the spreader with the handle on top and, lo and behold, all of the fertilizer came out in gigantic piles in four areas. I tried to spread it evenly all over the lawn, but that didn't work and I absolutely burned up that beautiful zoysia grass. Ultimately, it came back to life, but we always had four huge brown spots that were the result of my stupidity or carelessness.

Then came the best of the story.

I bought a new Toro lawn mower, a fancy deal, and I didn't know the first thing about how to operate it. But it was perfect for my zoysia grass and I was proud of it.

With Annette standing inside the kitchen and looking out the window, I cranked that baby and off I went. I was going in circles through the trees, mowing away, and I couldn't get the lawn mower stopped. It was flying and I was flying behind it.

Every time I passed the kitchen window I'd holler, "Annette, help me. Annette, I need ..." I wanted her to come out and show me how to stop the lawn mower. But, zoom, I was gone before I could tell her what I wanted. I don't know if she was laughing too hard to move, but she left me out there for what seemed like a lifetime going this way and going that way behind that thing.

Finally, Annette came outside. After she caught up with me, with the lawn mower still on the move, she pushed a little button and, boop, the engine cut off.

I was looking for a hole because I was extremely embarrassed.

Like I said, I didn't know anything about a lawn mower, but I figured I knew more about one than she did. That wasn't the case and we still laugh about that zoysia grass and that runaway Toro.

Annette laughs more than me about a couple of other things that happened on 15th Street.

One evening she caught me walking down the hallway on the tips of my toes, with my feet on the base boards. She said, "Winfrey, what on earth are you doing?" I told her I was trying to save our carpet, that I didn't want to wear it out. I was that proud of that wonderful house, the first one I owned or was making payments to own.

One afternoon, we had a major scare when our Volkswagen started rolling down the driveway. The boys were screaming that the car was getting away. We were helpless. We had to watch it roll into 15th Street, pick up steam going down a hill and over it and, finally, coming to rest in the woods. That thing could have killed somebody. I'm thankful to this day nobody got hurt.

Another great thing I remember about that house was a basketball goal I put up for the boys in the driveway. This was in 1967. Jim was about eight years old. Scott was about five. Annette was pregnant with Barry.

Looking back, there isn't any doubt I was a bully, not a wimp, while spending a lot of fine hours playing 21 with my sons, or hot tail as I remembered it from my childhood.

Also, I recall I always won and I would rub it in, really let them have it. I'd tell 'em I was the best player, there wasn't any way they could beat me. Annette got infuriated, lectured me because I ridiculed them so much, and Scott got so upset he'd come to the dinner table crying.

That's a natural reaction for a little boy. But maybe his dad was still a child, too.

I don't guess I was that much better than them, even when they were young, but I was smarter and more devious. If Jim and Scott had a chance to tie the game, I'd make a funny face or pull down their pants, do anything, really, to break their concentration.

We even had a chart on the refrigerator where we'd keep a record of wins and losses. Naturally, I was at the top of the standings because of a couple of reasons — I was stronger and I didn't give them a fair chance.

Wins didn't come quite so easily for the Alabama basketball program during that time. I've mentioned the 32 games we won from 1961 through 1963. Well, we followed that futility with 14-12, 17-9, 16-10, 13-13 and 10-16 records from 1964 through 1968. To say the Rocket Eight team the Crimson Tide had in 1956 was still the most popular among fans would be a gross understatement. That team coached by Johnny Dee had a 21-3 record and won the Southeastern Conference championship. The best we could do was finish in a tie for fifth place.

It seemed as if we were hopelessly plodding.

The simple truth is there were a lot of problems to overcome at Alabama, while Kentucky, Tennessee, Mississippi State and, later on, Vanderbilt weren't about to let what had been a proud program get back on its feet without a long hard struggle.

It's impossible for anybody to understand the agony we went through during the 1960s without knowing something about the history of the Alabama basketball program. So I'll attempt to give you some background material before I talk about the hard battle we fought to try to keep the Crimson Tide on track.

Not enough people know it, but Alabama basketball success goes back a long way, to the 1920s, 1930s and 1940s, basically when Hank Crisp, a football man, coached the team. He produced a 264-133 record from 1925 through 1942 and the 1946 season. He won the second Southeastern Conference championship in 1934, after having a good run through the Southern Conference.

The Alabama program ranks second to Kentucky in victories

among SEC members and as of this writing the third program in that regard, Tennessee, is about five dozen wins behind the Crimson Tide.

So it's a proud program and there are still a lot of people who talk about that great Rocket Eight team I mentioned earlier. For me, memories of that squad and Coach Johnny Dee are particularly poignant.

Coach Dee had come to Alabama for the 1953 season from Notre Dame and in 1956 put together an excellent team led by Jerry Harper, Leon Marlaire, George Linn and Jim Fulmer and Jim Lewis, who were from my hometown, Florence. They won the SEC championship and scored a resounding victory over Kentucky, 101-77, in Montgomery. They lost three tough games while traveling, at North Carolina, at St. John's and against Notre Dame in the Sugar Bowl Tournament in New Orleans.

I can recall Coach Dee speaking at my high school basketball banquet in Florence. Like me, he knew I wasn't good enough to play at Alabama, but he told me he would give me textbooks if I was interested in going to Tuscaloosa and trying out.

When I was at Arkansas Little Rock, I learned Coach Dee had cancer. He was living in Denver and we had a game scheduled out there. So I telephoned him and he came to our practice. We talked for a while and walked out of the gym with his son. It was the last time I saw him. It wasn't long before he died.

Johnny Dee was a great coach and a fine person. He was followed at Alabama in 1957 through 1960 by Dr. Eugene Lambert, who had been successful at Memphis State. They had a couple of decent years, 15-11 in 1957 and 17-9 in 1958, but ended up breaking even.

Still, Alabama basketball had long since been on the map, so to speak, particularly after Johnny Dee had that super season, his last before leaving to coach the Denver Truckers, a pro team.

Dr. Lambert gave me a break without knowing it when he and

Coach Paul "Bear" Bryant hired Hayden Riley as an assistant basketball coach. Actually, Coach Bryant was probably more interested in Coach Riley as a football recruiter because he was well liked and knew almost every high school coach in the state. Certainly, Coach Riley made great contributions to the rebuilding of the football program at The Capstone because many of the players he recruited became national champions.

As for me, Hayden Riley gave me the break of a lifetime when he became Alabama's head coach and hired me as a graduate assistant. That got my foot in the door, but it didn't put much money in my wallet. Basically, I had a scholarship to work on my Master's degree while coaching the freshman team. Thank heaven, I had a wife who was willing to work and was smart enough to make enough for us to make ends meet.

To be honest with you, I enjoyed coaching the freshman team during the 1961 season. Danny Ford, the future Alabama football star and national championship football coach at Clemson, played on our team that posted a 12-5 record, or something like that. The varsity had a harder time, going 7-18.

Just after the season ended, Leif Carlson, the former Michigan State player who was the top basketball assistant coach, decided to leave the Alabama program to go into private business.

Anyway, Coach Riley elevated me to assistant coach, for which I'm forever grateful. I was on the payroll, this time in earnest.

Coach Riley was a man I respected a great deal. He had integrity in all areas. He was one of the genuinely nice men in college athletics and he liked all aspects of it. As a former Alabama basketball player in 1947 and 1948, he knew a lot of people who supported the program and that enabled him to be a fantastic ambassador for the Crimson Tide.

I'll always consider Coach Riley a hero. He coached me. He gave me the chance to coach at Alabama. I owe him so much.

It was a little difficult for Coach Riley to take over the leadership of the Alabama basketball program, as it was for me several years later, and I did all I could to help him. He knew our sport, as some of his accomplishments against more famous coaches indicate, but I have wondered if he was too versatile for his own good. He knew football and how to recognize talent. He knew baseball and, later, coached the Crimson Tide team.

It was obvious to Coach Riley and everybody else that we were running short on talent in 1960. So our emphasis was recruiting. We had some good players left over from the years under Dr. Eugene Lambert, like Henry Hoskins and Larry Pennington, who were third team all-SEC in 1961, but we had to find a lot more like them to survive.

One super player we did get during that time was Bob Andrews, a center from Bridgeport, Illinois. He was with us from 1963 through 1965 and made first team all-SEC as a senior. He became the first Alabama player to accomplish that since 1958, when guard Jack Kubiszyn achieved such status.

Attempting to recruit of Bob Andrews and other players from Illinois and Indiana led me to meeting a good man, Roland Clark, who was a buddy of Coach Riley's from their days in the U.S. Navy. I'd stay at his house in Southern Illinois to save money and give me the chance see as many prospects as I could.

I was in Seymour, Indiana one night and had stopped at a little joint to get a hamburger. It was snowing like crazy and when I slammed the door my car keys flew off my index finger and landed in a thick blanket. I couldn't find them and, believe me, it was cold, windy, blustery and just plain awful.

Finally, I went inside the hamburger shop and asked the husband and wife owners if they had a dust pan I could borrow. I figured I'd be able to rake a row at a time until I found them. I raked and raked and raked without having any luck. When the woman came out to check on me, I said, "You know, ma'am, I'd probably have more luck if I turned on the headlights to the car."

Then she said, "That's right, sir, but how do you intend to do that with the doors locked?"

I couldn't help but laugh at my own stupidity, although I was miserable and stayed that way for a long time until I found those car keys.

Then there was the night Roland went with me to a game to watch a hot prospect. I was drinking a cola and he was chewing on a cigar. We were going fast down a two-lane highway when I looked up and saw a huge truck tire in the road. There was no way to avoid it. Blap, I hit it with the front tire on my side and the car jumped into the air like an Evil Knievel stunt. My cola went everywhere, all over the car, and Roland's cigar was busted and ruined.

We've laughed about that wild ride for years. But we weren't so amused when I was fighting the steering wheel trying to get that flying car under control.

Another great player, probably the best we got during the Foster Auditorium era, was Mike Nordholz. He was a lefthanded guard who lettered for us from 1966 through 1968. He could light it up. He scored 50 points in a loss to Southern Miss, 103-89, in 1967. That's a record for the program. He scored 1,394 points in three seasons, ranking 15th among all Crimson Tide players. He averaged 18.4 as a sophomore, 21.0 as a junior and 20.7 as a senior, definitely consistent numbers.

I'm smiling and not scowling because I had the chance to recruit Mike Nordholz and getting him out of Marietta, Georgia did wonders for my confidence. What is more, I'm sure the experience helped me become better in that vital part of coaching.

Rex Frederick, a former Auburn player, was an assistant coach at Georgia. He told me one day about how good this kid named Mike Nordholz was as a high school player. I picked up on the name, made a mental note and decided to check him out.

We worked hard on that recruitment. I believe we got him because we stayed after him day and night.

There were a few interesting anecdotes related to Mike's recruitment, one extremely somber and one particularly humorous, at least when my background is considered.

The first night I saw him play was the day John Kennedy was assassinated in Dallas, Texas. That was a sad time for everybody.

The last high school game I saw Mike play was in the Georgia State Tournament. His team was playing an opponent it had beaten four or five times that season. That's unusual in itself, but also hard for the team that has won so many times to do it again. He was fabulous that night and his team went on to win the championship.

Now for the funny part of his recruitment.

Mike had chronically bad ankles and his mother and father insisted he go to a college where coaches and trainers knew how to keep him healthy. I think I convinced them I knew how to do that and I think that's a major reason we got him.

So why is that funny?

Remember, I was the inexperienced and dumb Carbon Hill High School coach who almost crippled Herman Cook with the way I treated his ankle sprain.

So I flinched when C.M. Newton, who was coaching the freshman team in 1965, telephoned the basketball office after a game and said Mike Nordholz had suffered a sprained ankle during a game. The first thing I asked was if his ankles had been taped before the game. That was the case and I was relieved because I thought we were running the risk of a great player choosing to transfer to another program.

Watching players like Bob Andrews and Mike Nordholz perform made the hard times in Foster Auditorium somewhat enjoyable. Gary Elliott was another good one. We never were world beaters, not by any stretch, as our 102-104 record from 1961 through 1968 proves. But we had some quality players and some absolutely terrific wins during that time.

As I said earlier, we beat Tennessee and Kentucky back to back in Foster Auditorium. Their coaches were Ray Mears and Adolph Rupp, respectively, which should tell you something about the magnitude of those victories. The Kentucky team we beat in 1964 had a 21-6 record and won the SEC championship. Three years later, we beat Tennessee when the Volunteers were SEC champions.

Another memorable victory came over Mississippi State, 77-72, at Foster Auditorium in 1963. That was another SEC champion that Alabama defeated. In fact, we won three in a row over the Bulldogs in 1965 and 1966, so I guess you could say Coach Babe McCarthy considered Hayden Riley a thorn in his side.

Our problem during those years was consistency. We played several outstanding games. Also, we got drubbed several times.

Of course, a 3-13 record against Auburn was more painful than you can imagine. I'll talk more about that when discussing the old and yellowed "Beat Auburn" reminder I kept on my desk throughout my career and our success against them during the 1970s and the 1980s.

Before I move forward to a period of change in the Alabama basketball program, I'd be remiss if I didn't talk about the up close and personal view I had of one of the more significant days in the history of this state and this nation.

Students of history are familiar with that memorable day in the early 1960s when Alabama Governor George Wallace stood in a door at Foster Auditorium to keep Vivian Malone from becoming the first African-American to enroll at the University of Alabama. It was a symbolic gesture, that's all, his way of stating what then was his personal view of integration or, more accurately, I guess, his opinion that it was a decision for a state to make, not the federal government. Later in his life, he changed his viewpoint or at least softened his voice.

Regardless, the entire nation watched by way of television

when a representative from the United States Department of Justice read a statement and Governor Wallace read a statement before stepping aside and letting Miss Malone proceed through the registration process.

It was a carefully scripted event in history and I watched it unfold through a window at a building across the street that at that time housed the Alabama Athletics Department. I'll never forget that as long as I live — the limousines, the federal troops, the governor and, of course, Vivian Malone.

It doesn't take a genius to realize the positive impact that historical event at Foster Auditorium had on University of Alabama basketball and the sport as a whole.

CHAPTER FOUR

C.M. ... Integration ... and Success

A superb coaching staff: C.M. Newton, kneeling, with, left to right, John Bostick, Wimp Sanderson and Wendell Hudson

For as long as I live I'll never forget the strange feeling that swept over me when I heard a public address announcement during the Alabama High School State Basketball Tournament in 1968: "Coach Hayden Riley, please go see Coach Paul Bryant in his office."

There had been a lot of rumors, a lot of whispers and a lot of things said loudly about the University of Alabama basketball program for several months. Most of them dealt with staff changes and a redirection of the program.

I knew Coach Riley and Coach Bryant had been discussing what should be done for quite a while and I was wondering about my future.

The logic was we had just moved out of Foster Auditorium into Memorial Coliseum, a new home court, and Coach Bryant was looking for a way to give our program a fresh start. So for some reason a light came on in my head and I thought that meeting arranged by the public address announcer was about the future of my high school coach, current boss and, more importantly, cherished friend.

As for Coach Riley, he had done a good job as basketball coach and was thinking about moving into a new area within the athletics department. A consummate team player, as the saying goes, he had some ideas about where the basketball program should go and Coach Bryant respected his opinion.

We had one game remaining that season, at Auburn, and we were solidly entrenched in 10th place in Southeastern Conference standings. It was obvious our program was struggling and something had to happen to create enthusiasm and build momentum.

Coach Riley had the meeting with Coach Bryant, but he didn't tell me anything about it. It was a gut wrenching time, for sure, because I knew the winds of change were blowing and, as an assistant coach, my future might be unstable. Hayden had a lot to offer the athletics department. I thought I did, too, but I wasn't sure others agreed.

The night before we played at Auburn, a 73-69 loss, our sixth straight defeat, Coach Riley took me aside and told me it would be his last game. He said he had resigned as basketball coach and I found solace in the fact he had been reassigned and would take a more active role in the football operation.

As for me, I didn't know anything to do except keep working hard recruiting players and hope for the best. I was in the dark, so to speak, but I knew I was making inroads with some good prospects and needed to keep busting my fanny.

Meanwhile, the rumor mill kept churning and the name Charles Martin Newton kept popping up as the probable next head coach at Alabama. C.M. wasn't a stranger to me and others in Tuscaloosa because while on a sabbatical from Transylvania College he had been on campus during the fall of 1964 through the spring of 1965 working on his Master's degree and coaching our freshman team. He had made friends, which was easy for him to do because he's a personable man.

Looking back, I really think that year was the turning point that led to C.M. being named Alabama's coach. He was friends with Dr. Frank Rose, the university president, and Coach Bryant really liked him. That's a fairly powerful duo to have in your corner. Also, C.M. had played basketball at Kentucky under Coach Adolph Rupp when Coach Bryant was the football coach there.

A few other names surfaced as the possible next coach. But C.M. was the clear favorite.

C.M. has said Coach Bryant telephoned him, offered him the job and gave him less than a day to decide. He said he took the job, plus a pay cut, because he thought it would provide him with a good stepping stone. It worked out that way, no doubt, because since leaving Alabama in 1980 he has worked as an assistant commissioner in the Southeastern Conference Office, as Vanderbilt's coach and as Kentucky's athletics director. Now, incredulously, it's May of 2000 and Annette and I are about to attend his retirement party in Lexington, Kentucky. Sadly, this joyous occasion is coming a couple of months after Evelyn Newton, C.M.'s wonderful wife, died after a long fight with leukemia. Obviously, a lot of grand memories flashed through our minds when my wife and I attended her funeral.

When C.M. was hired, it was stated Coach Bryant wanted a levelheaded guy who might be able to restore the Alabama basketball program. But when fans heard the Crimson Tide was about to be led by a coach who was leaving somewhat obscure Transylvania College, the consensus opinion was Alabama was going to continue emphasizing football.

I had been on campus a while and I knew we really wanted to have a good program. So I wasn't among those who were doubting or laughing. I was worrying because I didn't know if I would have a job.

Another thing interesting about that time of change is while Coach Riley was running the basketball program I received a letter from John Bostick, who at that time was an outstanding coach at Gadsden High School. He said he wanted to step up to the college level and inquired about the situation at Alabama. I wrote him and said a lot was going on and I didn't have any idea what might happen in the immediate future.

When C.M. arrived on campus, I was still recruiting. I was working on players like Alan House in Birmingham, Alabama, David Williams in Pensacola, Florida, Doug Gamble in New Brockton, Alabama and several others. I'll admit it was tough trying to stay in the fold with some prospects because it was a difficult circumstance and we didn't spend much money going out to visit those guys.

I asked C.M. if there was a chance I'd be able to stay on the staff. He told me Coach Bryant had told him it would be best if he got a new staff, that he felt a clean sweep would probably be the thing to do. C.M. said he would talk to Coach Bryant again, but he didn't know if I'd be retained.

It was a low period for me and my family. I felt hurt because I had put so much effort into it and continued to do so. But I decided I should stay on the road recruiting, keep working hard, and there were many times when C.M. accompanied me. We signed some good players. We signed some bad players. But we signed some people who a few years later really got the program going again.

Ultimately, I asked C.M. to let me stay. I was honest with him, told him how much it meant to me to be a part of Alabama basketball. After talking to Coach Bryant some more, he decided to retain me. Obviously, I'm indebted to him for that. He kept an assistant coach who had been a part of an unsuccessful tenure. That doesn't happen much. I'm grateful it did that time.

C.M. added Jock Sutherland to the staff. He was a highly successful coach at Lafayette High School in Lexington, Kentucky, the heart of some great basketball, and it became obvious we would work that part of the country while recruiting.

The C.M. Newton Era didn't get off to a rousing start. We won 12 games total in 1969 and 1970, 4-20 and 8-18, and we were 10-16 in 1971. The critics were roaring. But we had some good talent coming in every year. In fact, that first season we had freshmen who could have played on the varsity if NCAA rules had allowed it at that time.

Also, after I mentioned the opportunity to get a good high school coach on board with us, C.M. hired John Bostick as an assistant coach. That started a long run of continuity for the program with the three of us on the practice floor together and on the bench during games.

Let me talk a little more about the trying times, 1969 through 1971, before I get into the good times that started in 1972 and have lasted.

We lost the first game in 1969 at Duke, 86-48, and as I recall we went a lifetime before we scored. I remember C.M. turning toward me and saying, "Has anybody ever been shut out in college basketball?"

Auburn beat us twice that season, continuing the frustration.

We lost seven in a row at one point and six in a row at one point of the 1970 season. Auburn swept us again, winning 121-78 down there, making our record against the intrastate rival 3-17 for the most recent decade.

Also, there is something wrong when the highlight of your season is watching an opposing player score 69 points against you. That happened on February 7, 1970, when we beat LSU in Memorial Coliseum, 106-104, and the wonderful Pete Maravich put a big dent in our defense. A truly magnificent player, he made 26 of 57 field goal attempts and 17 free throws.

The margins of defeat tightened in 1971, but Kentucky, Tennessee and Auburn all swept us and anybody who wasn't at practice and saw our players getting better day by day had reason to believe the Alabama basketball program wasn't going anywhere.

I knew otherwise because I realized we had made a commitment to recruiting African-American players, or minorities, and in Wendell Hudson we had a special one on campus. As it worked out, his success on and off the basketball court led to a long line of superstars that kept coming to Tuscaloosa. For every good player Auburn and other programs got in our state, the Crimson Tide got five. That's how you win.

I didn't have much to do with recruiting Wendell during the

spring of 1970. C.M. made a strong commitment for taking long and hard looks at minority players and, in the case of Wendell, he and Jock Sutherland did most of the recruiting. If I contributed anything, it came during a conversation we had after I had been to Birmingham to watch a high school game. C.M. asked me how the talent looked. I told him he better go pick a minority player or two of his choosing because they were playing above the rim and we needed that.

The timing was perfect because in 1970 Coach Bryant began recruiting African-American football players, with defensive end John Mitchell and halfback Wilbur Jackson leading the way.

I can't say enough about Wendell. Not only was he a nice young man, he was courageous, really showed a lot of intestinal fortitude. He quietly went about the business of integrating our athletics department and his fellow students really took to him. He was softspoken and always smiling. I'm sure he realized the significance of what he, John Mitchell and Wilbur Jackson were doing, but not once did he give the appearance of thinking he was important. He just wanted to go to class and, of course, play basketball.

The team we put on the court in 1972 should have an honored place in Alabama basketball history. It was a far cry from The Wendell Hudson Show, plus a few others. We had several fine players, such as senior guards Bobby Lynch and Jimmy Hollon, senior center Alan House, senior forward David Williams, junior guard Paul Ellis, who was strong coming off the bench, junior forward Glenn Garrett and sophomore guard Raymond Odums. We didn't have much depth, not from a quality standpoint at that time, but we were starting to develop the type pipeline any coach would want — seniors, juniors, sophomores and freshmen in waiting.

Among the freshmen in 1972 were guard Charles Cleveland and forward Johnny Dill. Through a stroke of good fortune, the changing of NCAA rules to allow freshmen to play on the varsity in 1973, our position was improved because we were recruiting a high school star who we knew would make an instant impact.

Does the name Leon Douglas ring a bell?

But I'm not moving forward until I give 1972 a thorough rehashing because that was the breakthrough season for Alabama basketball. The 18-8 record is only part of the story. The SEC record was 13-5, good enough for third place behind Tennessee and Kentucky, who shared the title with 14-4 records. The home record was 13-0, which created a lot of enthusiasm, particularly among students.

What is more, the 1972 team lost four of its first seven games, then won 10 of its next 12. The two losses came at Tennessee, 79-77, and at Kentucky, 77-74. Later in the year we beat Tennessee, 72-67, on Saturday night and Kentucky, 77-74, on Monday night and support for Alabama basketball reached its highest peak since the Rocket Eight in 1956.

Deservedly, C.M. was named SEC Coach of the Year by the *Associated Press* and *United Press International.*

Oh, do not let me forget we defeated Auburn twice that season, 89-66 at home and 79-78 on the road. Our intrastate rival beat us one time the remainder of the 1970s, 76-70 down there in 1976. The tables had turned and I was among the delighted.

Obviously, the 1972 season was enjoyable. But the 1973 season made all of us more ecstatic. We had a 22-8 record, finished second to Kentucky by a game in the SEC championship race and made that aforementioned memorable trip to the National Invitation Tournament.

Wendell Hudson capped his career as SEC Player of the Year, the first in the history of the program, and Charles Cleveland, who was about as accurate shooting from almost midcourt as he was shooting layups, joined him on the all-SEC team. Ray Odums, a great playmaking guard and a defensive terror, as well as one of the hardest working players we had, was second team all-SEC.

Wendell was phenomenal all season. He averaged 20.7 points and 12.1 rebounds per game. He made 56.7 percent of his field goal attempts. If those aren't player of the year stats, show me something more impressive.

Alabama lost five conference games in 1973 and three of them were by two points or less. The killers were to Kentucky at home, 95-93, and at Tennessee, 72-71, when Paul Ellis got knocked down while attempting a shot from the corner at the buzzer and no foul was called — a really bad blown call at Stokely Athletics Center in Knoxville. We were that close to winning the third SEC championship in the history of the program.

That type hard luck followed that team to the 1973 NIT. After beating Manhattan and Minnesota in the first round and the quarterfinal round at Madison Square Garden, we lost to Virginia Tech, 74-73, in the semifinals. We got drilled by North Carolina in the consolation game, 88-69, but that did little to diminish what had been accomplished during an incredible season.

Also, with talented players stockpiled, we were anxious to get the next season started. We had Charles Cleveland, Ray Odums, Leon Douglas and Johnny Dill returning. We had T.R. Dunn, Rickey Brown and Charles "Boonie" Russell, a junior college transfer, coming in.

To say the University of Alabama Athletics Department was an exciting place to be during that time is a gross understatement. The football team had produced 11-1 and 10-2 records in 1971 and 1972, after falling on hard times in 1969 and 1970, and it was about to produce an 11-1 record in 1973. Coach Bryant had made a commitment to all sports and had told Coach Sam Bailey, his chief assistant athletics director, to bring everybody up to football and basketball standards. No longer did Tennessee own the SEC All-Sports Trophy because nobody was winning like the Crimson Tide during that time.

That had a nice ring to it, bring everybody up to football and basketball standards, and the Sanderson family was as happy as ever. We had moved into a wonderful house in Woodland Hills, where we stayed two decades, Jim, Scott and Barry were growing up in a hurry and taking active interests in basketball and the Newtons, the Bosticks and the Sandersons were dear friends.

As much as I hated leaving that great little red brick house on 15th Street — in fact, we still own it — the house we built in Woodland Hills was perfect for the boys. They each had a bedroom. They had a nice yard. They had a real neighborhood of friends. We put up a basketball goal so the hot tail games could continue.

I was into softball, too, playing for the church team, and I loved to take Jim, Scott and Barry to games with me. When they were over, they would run the basepaths, sliding at every stop, and, as little boys do, they'd be filthy when we left the park to go home. I've still got great memories of those summer evenings when there wasn't any constant pressure to win and win and win on the basketball court.

Actually, the pressure was subsiding, if only a bit, because we all knew we had finally moved along the Alabama basketball program and had made great strides in terms of statewide interest and national exposure.

The interest among high school players, including prospects, allowed us to have a bonanza time recruiting. The marque players in our state wanted to be a part of the Crimson Tide program and that allowed us to get the best of the batch. You can imagine how they felt when they saw pictures of Alabama players packing up for an extended trip to play in the NIT.

In this era the NIT doesn't mean much because there are 64 teams in the NCAA Tournament. But during the 1970s, when the NCAA Tournament field was much smaller, the NIT was a prestigious event. Also, the entire event was staged at Madison

Square Garden, with only sixteen superb teams invited, and that meant kids from the backwoods of Alabama would get to spend a week or ten days in the Big Apple. That excited me. There wasn't any doubt it excited them.

Times were good in 1973.

Things got better for all of us in 1974, when we posted a 22-4 record and tied Vanderbilt for the SEC championship. The Commodores got the berth in the NCAA Tournament, which was much smaller at the time, because they beat us twice, 73-72 in Nashville and 67-65 in Tuscaloosa. Our only other conference loss came at Florida, 64-61, in that darn cracker box called Alligator Alley, and the other loss was to powerful St. John's, 72-67, in the Connecticut Classic.

I'll help you with the math. There were four losses by a total of 11 points. That's not far from perfection and I don't think there are many people outside of Nashville who believed we didn't have a team good enough to go a long way in the NCAA Tournament. That team won at Kentucky, 94-71, which is not easily done, and I think it could've made it to the Elite Eight or Final Four.

The SEC during those years was easy to define. There were the haves, Alabama, Kentucky, Tennessee and Vanderbilt, and the have nots, all of the others. Some of the have nots were hard to beat at home, like Florida in Alligator Alley, but the best players were landing on the campuses of the haves and we were thankful to be among that group.

I've talked about some of the players who had entered our program, like Leon Douglas, who could do anything a coach wanted him to and was willing to work at it, and the impressive list kept growing. As an example, T.R. Dunn from Birmingham's West End High School might have been the most complete player we had. He played as a freshman in 1974, a leader from the start. We added Anthony Murray, a lightning quick guard, to that list in 1975, his freshman season, and, suddenly, we had the finest array of talent in Crimson Tide history.

Let me tell you more about those players.

Leon was quiet and intelligent. At 6-foot-10, he was an ominous force near the basket. He had a flair about him, not so flashy, which takes me back to the official recruiting visit he made to Alabama in 1972.

I don't think I was there because I was probably away scouting our next opponent. If not, I was in the dressing room at halftime. Anyway, they introduced Leon to the crowd and he walked to midcourt amid a thunderous standing ovation, gave everybody a big grin and doffed a cabby cap he was wearing.

That was a sign of the times. Alabama people were getting into basketball again.

T.R. was much quieter. He was more reserved. Heck, he had a wife and young son, Little T, who shared the dressing room with us on many occasions. I'll never forget the little guy wrestling with a basketball as his father granted newspaper reporters interviews after many of our games.

Another thing about T.R. is he was a silky smooth player, the best I ever saw when it came to gathering garbage, such as a rebound loose on the court or an errant pass. He was so unselfish he shot only when he needed to, when a teammate wasn't open, and we could count on him getting 10 points a game. I bet if you asked sports writers who covered our teams during those years to name the most polite, humble and sincere guy on our squads they would tell you T.R. Dunn.

Anthony "Amp" Murray, had more flair on the court, but was just as softspoken as T.R. off the court. He grew up the hard way in Fairfield, just outside Birmingham, and there was such a richness about his spirit and his will to excel that it filtered into all of us.

"Amp" literally played as hard as anybody could, until his lungs ached, his head bowed and his shoulders dropped. But if you gave him two minutes of rest, he was back at it, with a vengeance, and he took more pride in stopping an opponent from scoring than he did making a basket.

In many ways Anthony Murray epitomized the players we had at Alabama during those years. I'll never forget his effort, which I'll talk more about.

They were Alabama reared and they were Alabama proud, most of the young men who led us into the 1975 and 1976 seasons, and that came through crystal clear.

The Crimson Tide repeated as SEC champion in 1975, sharing the title with Kentucky, and made it to the NCAA Tournament. The Wildcats beat us twice, both times by five points, so I can't argue with their claim of superiority. But we had a 22-5 record, 15-3 in the conference, so we weren't second fiddle by much.

The NCAA Tournament experience was grand, although not totally successful. We went to Tempe, Arizona and lost to Arizona State, 97-94, in the first round. Leon Douglas was unbelievable that afternoon, scoring 29 points and grabbing 21 rebounds. T.R. scored 21 points, which was unusual because he rarely took many shots.

I've mentioned what we accomplished in 1976, making it to the NCAA Tournament Sweet 16. But that team deserves a little more consideration because it posted a 23-5 record and won the SEC championship.

Interestingly, we started the 1976 season by hosting the Soviet Union National Team in an exhibition game. That was a talented outfit made up of gold medalists and they beat us by one point, 63-62, in a memorable contest.

The real losses were hard to swallow. Princeton beat us by two, Florida beat us by one, Tennessee beat us by six, Kentucky beat us by five and Indiana beat us by five in the second round of the NCAA Tournament.

We opened play in the NCAA Tournament in Dayton, Ohio and defeated North Carolina, 79-64. That was a stunning performance by Alabama against a team that featured Walter Davis, Mitch Kupchak and Phil Ford. They put a dozen players on the court that afternoon and we used seven.

But our seven were special. The starters were Leon Douglas, Reggie King, Rickey Brown, T.R. Dunn and Anthony Murray. Our backups were Keith McCord and Greg McElveen.

Leon scored 35 points and got 17 rebounds. Meanwhile, Kupchak scored eight and got 12. "Amp" scored 13, a high number for him, and, as the star of the game he held Ford to two points. That was a spectacular defensive effort.

I can't go another line without talking about Reggie King, although that super player and wonderful person will receive more attention later. He was fresh out of high school in 1976, but he was a star even while playing a specific role in a fairly experienced lineup. He scored 13 points and got 11 rebounds against North Carolina. He was on his way to rewriting the Alabama record book.

Reggie moved like a turtle off the court, acting as if he was lazy, but he moved like a rabbit on the court. He had a gigantic smile. He was a coach's dream, really, and might be the most popular Crimson Tide player in the history of the program among fans. He was a major reason we got to that showdown with Indiana.

The Hoosiers, coached by Bobby Knight, were unbeaten and they had an awesome lineup. Kent Benson was their center. Scott May and Tom Abernathy were their forwards. Bob Wilkerson and Quinn Buckner were their guards.

As I said earlier, we took them to the wire, although Leon and Reggie had off nights when it came to scoring. We had the lead by one point and were milking the clock as they used a passive defense. This was inside the final two minutes. The crowd at LSU was going crazy, sensing an upset of a team everybody thought was unbeatable. Then one of our players who was simply holding the basketball as the seconds ticked away dropped the darn thing.

It hit his thigh or knee and bounced forward. One of their guards grabbed it and started a fastbreak that ended with them scoring a layup basket. We had to go on the attack, they stopped us and they scored again.

Just like that, what would have been the greatest Alabama basketball victory in history became one of the more agonizing defeats.

It's interesting that our program started a bit of a decline after that disappointment in Baton Rouge, Louisiana. It began slowly because we got off to a 14-0 start in 1977, before losing at Tennessee, and the record that season was 25-6. We went 17-10 in 1978, 11-7 in the conference, 22-11 in 1979, 11-7 in the conference, and 18-12 in 1980, 12-6 in the conference.

Probably the most memorable game during those four seasons was a 78-62 win over Kentucky in Tuscaloosa. The Wildcats had a 30-2 record that season and won the national championship. They had the twin towers, Mike Phillips and Rick Robey, two giants under the basket.

Well, we fooled them and we whipped them. We started three guards, an extremely small lineup, pressed on defense and ran the court on offense. It was like a mole hill battling Mount Everest — and it worked.

Meanwhile, our fans were erratic, showing up for big games and staying home for little games, and that really started getting to C.M.. John and I didn't understand it, either, but the head coach was really frustrated.

Coaching can be a thankless occupation and C.M. felt underappreciated in a major way. The football program, for all its glory, contributed to that because Alabama roared through the 1970s, setting a NCAA record for wins during a decade and claiming three national championships. His disappointment came to a head midway though the 1980 season when we won back to back games at LSU and at Kentucky, in front of packed arenas, and came home to play our next game against Georgia in front of a sparse crowd. I'm telling you Memorial Coliseum wasn't half full that night, with probably 6,500 or so in attendance..

I think that was the crowning blow that led to C.M.'s decision to resign at the end of that season. He had talked about his frustration a lot and it really started rearing its head at that time.

CHAPTER FIVE

The 1980s: A Decade to Remember

A young Wimp Sanderson displayed a highly competitive demeanor while leading the Crimson Tide basketball program

I don't recall the date, but not long after the University of Alabama basketball season ended in March of 1980, C.M. Newton and I were visiting in his office. He said he had talked with Evelyn, his wife, and they had decided the time had come for him to resign as coach. They concluded he was tired and wasn't enjoying the job like he had in the past.

I think an underlying reason for C.M. deciding enough was enough were a couple of people in the athletics department who rubbed him the wrong way. I don't think he felt like continuing to fight the battles they presented.

There wasn't any doubt he was weary from the grind. He had done an excellent job of getting the basketball program back on solid ground and the hard work had taken a physical and mental toll. He might have been burned out, pure and simple.

C.M. told me that day he couldn't guarantee me the job he was leaving. He said he would talk to Coach Paul "Bear" Bryant and Coach Sam Bailey about it, even recommend me to them, but he didn't know what direction the University of Alabama would follow while searching for a new head coach.

I had been for a few interviews by that time, all of them coming during the 1970s, but nothing had worked out to my liking. I visited with the folks at Iowa State. They hired Lynn Nance. I went to Ole Miss and they hired Bob Weltlich. I went to Mississippi State and they hired Ron Greene. At one point I had been offered the job at Southern Miss, but decided against taking it. I visited with the folks at South Alabama when they were starting that program. They ended up hiring Rex Frederick.

The opportunities had been sparse and I didn't have much

experience looking, so I didn't know how it would work out at Alabama. I thought Coach Bryant and Coach Bailey felt like I had done a decent job for the program. However, I knew there was a chance they might want to bring in a name coach with an impressive resume.

At about that time, Tennessee Tech contacted me about a vacancy. I went to Cookeville and visited with the folks there and they seemed extremely interested in hiring me. Not knowing what might happen at Alabama, I continued to show interest in that job, sort of biding my time before a decision had to be made.

The Final Four was in Indianapolis that year and, as usual, I planned to go up there to watch the three games and socialize with fellow coaches. C.M. went up ahead of me to attend some meetings for a couple of days and secured a suite at a hotel.

My telephone rang just as I was walking out of the door to go to the airport for the flight to Indianapolis. It was the president or athletics director at Tennessee Tech, the president, I think, and he told me they were ready to announce my appointment as coach. In fact, he said he wanted to do that in a day or two.

I told him I wanted to get to Indianapolis, talk to C.M. a little more about the Alabama job and then decide what direction I should take.

When I arrived in Indianapolis, I told C.M. I had just been offered the Tennessee Tech job. He said, "What's your thinking?" I said, "My thinking is I'm going to roll the dice and go for the Alabama job."

C.M. reiterated he couldn't guarantee me anything at Alabama, that there was a chance I wouldn't get the job.

I told him I understood that, that I had been there 20 years and if I didn't get the job as head coach I'd pack up my belongings in a paper sack and get out of there by nightfall.

So I called the administration at Tennessee Tech and told them I was going to roll the dice at Alabama, that I had been there too long.

I really appreciated Tennessee Tech's interest in me because I hadn't had many opportunities. They quickly hired Tom Deason, an assistant coach at Tennessee, and I kept working on getting the Alabama job.

It was a close call. I almost went to Cookeville, Tennessee instead of staying in Tuscaloosa, Alabama.

I had some hurdles to clear, some large ones. C.M. had left the program in good shape, with some good players coming back, and I knew there were some members of the alumni across the state who weren't going to be supportive of the Alabama program unless a coach with an impressive track record was hired. They didn't want the Crimson Tide to run the risk of returning to mediocrity by hiring a lifelong assistant coach who had basically focused on recruiting.

On the flip side, there were some members of the alumni in Birmingham who were in my corner. They were strong voices and I knew they would call Coach Bryant and Coach Bailey and express their support.

It was a wait and see proposition for what seemed like forever and it was such an emotional time I can't recall the details of what happened before I was hired.

One thing I do remember with ease is how tough that first season was for me. From the first day of practice in October of 1980 until the final game of the season in the National Invitation Tournament I was on a rollercoaster, up and down, and as tight as a bass fiddle.

I convinced John Bostick to stay with me, which was a blessing, although he really didn't like working under my direction much and left after only one season.

I guess I was hard to work for and play for because I'm more intense than most competitors and, of course, I brought an entirely different personality to leadership. I pushed players hard, demanded a lot, and I took losses in a terrible way. I definitely had a I'll show the world approach and the pressure was immense.

As for the players on that first team, it was a mixed bag of those who liked to work hard and those who didn't like working up much of a sweat. That was sort of normal for that time period because young men were changing a lot, in some cases taking an "I" attitude instead of the "we" attitude that had served us so well during the 1970s.

Our only senior that season, at least among those who played much, was Ken "Silk" Johnson, a forward from Phenix City. He was from the old school, if you want to put it that way, and played for the love of the game.

Our juniors were Eddie Phillips, Phillip Lockett, Maurice Myers and Eddie Adams. Our sophomores were Mike Davis and Cliff Windham. Our freshmen were Eric Richardson and Terry Williams.

All of those people contributed. Some were fun to coach. Some were hard to coach, to even understand.

We got off to a fast start, 7-0, but were up and down the rest of the way, ultimately finishing with an 18-11 overall record and a 10-8 Southeastern Conference record. There were a few excruciating losses, like by one point to Tennessee in overtime, two points to Vanderbilt and Auburn and three points to LSU.

We lost to Georgia in the first round of the SEC Tournament, 88-80, and were delighted to get a berth in the NIT. That was a blessing for more than one reason because I had a couple of conversations during the postseason that really helped me.

We played and defeated St. John's, 73-69, on its home court in the first round of the NIT, at Nassau Coliseum on Long Island. In the dressing room just before that game I asked John Bostick why our players despised me so much. He was blatantly honest with me when he said, "They don't think you care about them."

That was something to chew on, food for thought.

Also, on that trip I had the opportunity to visit at some length with Lou Carnesecca, the great St. John's coach. I talked to Lou about some of the problems I had experienced with players that made the first year so difficult. He shared problems he had experienced throughout his career and said he had several to overcome with his current team. I guess there is comfort in misery because that conversation made me feel somewhat better.

Beating St. John's on its home court was good tonic, too, a confidence builder. We lost to Duke on its home court in the second round of the NIT, 75-70, in Durham, North Carolina. A loss is a loss, always painful, but there wasn't any disgrace associated with that one.

As most people know, it's difficult to follow a successful person. That's what I faced that season after what C.M. Newton had accomplished. Some coaches quit because they're losing. C.M. left after winning a bunch of games, after producing a 211-123 record from 1969 through 1980.

So the pressure was on and I felt it. We didn't get to the NCAA Tournament that first year, just to the NIT, and I would've been much more content had I known we would eventually make it to the NCAA Tournament 10 times in the 12 years I had the job.

But I've never considered myself as the reason for that type success. It was our players who accomplished that and I'm still convinced having good players often gets confused with good coaching.

We worked hard recruiting and we got good players. The foundation had been established in the state of Alabama and we solidified it. That enabled us to have the type program we wanted during the 1980s.

It's interesting that my biggest problem in 1981 was a star player. He led our team in scoring with 17 points per game, led us in rebounding with 9.8 per game and, in my opinion, led the world in creating team dissention.

The player didn't like my coaching style. Nor did he like me as a person. He called secret meetings with some players before practices and created discord. He didn't want to cooperate. At one point during the season he called C.M. to complain about me. He gave his former coach a list of numerous things his present coach was doing wrong. He said nobody on the team wanted to play for me.

Somehow, that team got through a rough ride and had some success — and better days were directly in front of the Alabama basketball program.

In some circles C.M. continues to get credit for winning those 18 games in 1981 because everybody said it was his team that won over Kentucky during the regular season and St. John's during the NIT.

In fact, I can laugh now about a telephone conversation I had with C.M. during the rigors of that first year. As we chatted, I remember saying, "C.M., you might as well come back to Tuscaloosa and reclaim this job because everybody around here thinks it's your team I'm trying to coach."

CHAPTER SIX

Athletics Directors: Different Types

After two technical fouls, Wimp Sanderson has a few words with official Dale Kelley during a Crimson Tide victory over LSU in 1984

Before I go romping gleefully through the 1980s and part of the 1990s, when the University of Alabama basketball program gave me the happiest professional period in my lifetime, let me tell you a few things about how the athletics department in Tuscaloosa, Alabama operated during my 32 years of employment. That's the only way you will be able to fully understand the highs and lows I had while coaching the Crimson Tide from 1981 through 1992.

Unless you've been out of the country for the most recent two decades, you're aware of how the Alabama Athletics Department has resembled a made for television soap opera since Coach Paul "Bear" Bryant died in 1983. Well, I can tell you there were good times, with great leadership, and some bad times.

So let's discuss the changes the Alabama Athletics Department went through during a tumultuous decade.

I've already told you what Coach Bryant meant to the athletics department, our basketball program and to me personally. He was a strong leader, totally in charge, and as I look back on him as an athletics director I really have enormous respect for the way he got things done.

Football was his game, the one he coached, and that's where he placed emphasis after arriving on campus in 1958. That was a natural course of action because the football program needed rebuilding, which he accomplished, and the football program was the only one that made money.

Coach Bryant maintained that position until Alabama football had regained national prominence and, as I've said, he saw our basketball program had a chance to contribute financially.

As an athletics director, Coach Bryant was from the old school. He ran a tight budget. As an example, he didn't pay basketball coaches much. Nor did he pay his assistant football coaches much. It was his belief that they would be able to make a lot of money later if they worked hard under him and advanced in the profession. Certainly that worked out in most cases.

Coach Bryant was an ideal athletics director because he cared about his people, he loved the University of Alabama and, by golly, he was a strong leader who commanded respect.

I don't think any of us realized the ups and downs the Alabama Athletics Department would go through after his death. I'm convinced the transition from him to a new leader would have been much more smooth had he not died because he planned to stay on the job for about six months to help the program retain focus.

I was at about the midpoint of my third season as head basketball coach when Coach Bryant died. Ray Perkins, the new football coach, was about a month away from the start of his first spring practice on campus.

I'll talk about Ray Perkins the football coach in the next chapter, when I discuss all of them in some detail. But I'll tell you now he was a good athletics director, a strong supporter of our basketball program and my family, after rising to that position in a strange manner.

After Coach Bryant died, Ray was on the selection committee formed to pick the next athletics director. He decided he wanted the job, in addition to his duties as football coach. I know that's how it happened because after the process was under way I was added to the selection committee.

I don't think there was anybody else other than Ray we seriously considered. A lot of basketball coaches jump up and down because the football coach is the athletics director, but that wasn't the case with me. I was extremely supportive of Ray and I'm glad he got the job.

Similarly, Ray was a little different than most football coaches. He wanted our basketball program to be successful throughout his term at Alabama, 1983 through 1986. He wanted every Crimson Tide sport to be a winner. He wasn't concerned about the growing popularity of basketball on campus, nor about my popularity among fans.

I'll give you a good example of the support he gave our program and me.

After we made it to the NCAA Tournament Sweet 16 in 1985, I had programs that contacted me about making a move. One of them was South Carolina, which interested me, and I went to visit with them.

After I returned to Tuscaloosa, I went to see Ray and told him about my interview, that maybe the time had come for me to make a change. After all, I had been at Alabama for a quarter of a century. To put that meeting in better perspective, you've got to remember he had just come off a dismal football season, a 5-6 record, and there was a lot of pressure on him.

Ray was extremely cordial, as always with me, and he made me feel wanted. He acted as if he didn't want me to leave. He was able to get me a raise in salary. He did some other things that helped my position. I don't know what else an athletics director could do in that situation.

Ray was a fierce competitor who wanted the best for Alabama. Also, he was a tireless worker who would get on an airplane and stay gone for days trying to help the athletics department.

Ray upgraded the facilities immensely, something that was needed badly. He started the renovation and expansion of Bryant-Denny Stadium. To this day he maintains Alabama should have the largest football stadium in the nation simply because it's Alabama, the best program in the nation.

Everybody knows Ray rubbed some people the wrong way when he initiated change. Part of the reason is he's a little difficult for some people to get to know. He's a matter of fact type guy, mostly business, and he took some strong and at times harsh stances while leading the athletics department. But, again, he made his decisions based on what he thought was best for Alabama, his alma mater.

In summary, Ray had some enemies, a bunch among so called Alabama supporters. I wasn't one of them.

I was in Kansas City, Missouri when I heard Ray might be making a return to pro football, going to Tampa Bay to work for Hugh Culverhouse. After that deal was finalized, seemingly fast, I telephoned Ray and asked what I needed to do to get more control of our basketball program. We were having success, really moving forward, and I didn't want to see our support diminished.

Ray told me he thought Steve Sloan might become the next Alabama athletics director, that he thought Dr. Joab Thomas, the school president, was leaning in that direction. So I arranged a visit with Dr. Thomas at his house with the idea of discussing the future.

Dr. Thomas had a lot on him at the time. He was searching for a football coach and he was searching for an athletics director. The program was starting all over again, or it seemed, just four years after Coach Bryant had passed away.

Dr. Thomas is a cordial man and was always nice to me. We visited about several things and I told him I was interested in getting the basketball program a little more under my jurisdiction.

Eventually, we talked about the next athletics director and he confirmed that it might be Steve Sloan. C.M. Newton was mentioned, too, but he was having some physical problems during that time while at Vanderbilt.

Dr. Thomas told me a few years earlier he had telephoned Steve when he was at Duke to ask if he had interest in becoming Alabama's football coach if the position became open. Steve told him no, but added he would be interested in the athletics director position if that opportunity presented itself.

Dr. Thomas had made a decision to split the two positions, to have someone other than the football coach as athletics director, so we talked about people under consideration for the coaching job. He mentioned Danny Ford, Howard Schnellenberger and Bill Curry, plus a couple of other people, and it seemed to me he was leaning toward Bill Curry, who was at Georgia Tech.

It was a little peculiar how the process was working. Dr. Thomas was going to hire Bill Curry as football coach and then hire Steve Sloan as athletics director. Normally, that's reversed.

Anyway, Steve became my next boss and he was a super athletics director. I don't think there's anybody I've respected and cared more about than him. I know there are people who feel otherwise, some heavy hitters, but I'm here to tell you he was great for the program and he got a bad deal.

The way he was handled and ultimately cut loose in 1988 was a total disgrace.

Steve got blamed by some influential Alabama graduates and other so called supporters of the program because Auburn Coach Pat Dye wanted to move the home and home football rivalry to that campus.

Steve could not have stopped that if he had stood in the school house door with a machine gun in his hands. The contract at Legion Field in Birmingham was over. Auburn had every contractual right to play its home games with Alabama at Jordan-Hare Stadium. It was an open and shut case. For Alabama power brokers to think they could have changed that was foolish.

Some of those power brokers said Steve Sloan was soft in his dealings with rivals. That's ridiculous. He's a smart guy and a wonderful person. He's one of the finest football players who ever attended the University of Alabama and he was an outstanding leader for the athletics department. I honestly can't find one thing critical to say about the man. He wasn't soft at all, although he was compassionate.

Steve had a couple of assistant athletics directors who talked about him all the time behind his back. They treated him like a dog, spilled rumors into the streets. But he kept them around because he was so nice and cared about them and their families.

People should have been that fair dealing with him because it's a dishonor what happened to Steve Sloan. How he was dismissed as athletics director points out how mysteriously driven some people can be when trying to better themselves.

The first wave of trouble for Steve came when Dr. Joab Thomas resigned to assume the presidency of Penn State University. He lost a good friend that day, a man who had been supportive of him and Coach Bill Curry, who was under fire in a major way.

Steve was catching flak from so called Alabama supporters on a couple of points, one for the dissatisfaction they had with Bill Curry and one for the fear they had of going to Auburn to play a football game.

Steve made an appearance in front of the Red Elephant Club in Montgomery. During his speech he talked about scheduling, specifically finding the right balance between home games and away games. He pointed out that Auburn had played nine home games one season and he said something like, "After talking with Auburn, I've concluded it isn't in our best interest to have that many games on campus in one year."

As soon as those words left his mouth, Aaron Aranov, a University of Alabama Board of Trustees member, got up and left the room in a huff, obviously mad about something. After the speech had ended, as Steve was preparing to leave, Aranov stopped him and asked why he would confer with Auburn about scheduling. He bluntly said Alabama didn't have to confer with Auburn about anything.

Obviously, Aranov thought that was a show of weakness, when in reality Steve was pointing out the dangers associated with scheduling in an unwise manner.

When it came time for the next Alabama president to be appointed, several people attempted to get the job, including Dr. Roger Sayers, who was a longtime vice president who wanted to step up.

In the process of being interviewed, Sayers was told by Aranov that the first thing he would be expected to do if he became president is fire Steve Sloan. He became president of the University of Alabama. A good athletics director and a superb gentleman was on his way out.

I'll never forget walking into Steve's office one morning and taking a seat for a friendly chat. I asked him how he was doing and he said, "Coach, things aren't good. I've just been to see Dr. Sayers and he had some hard things to say. I could've closed my eyes while he was talking and heard the voice of Aaron Aranov."

Then Steve said, "I think Dr. Sayers is going to terminate me within the next two weeks."

I dropped my teeth. I couldn't believe it.

Everything was built around Steve Sloan not being able to stop Auburn from playing Alabama on its campus.

Everything was built around Steve Sloan being soft.

Everything was built around Steve Sloan playing too much golf and not working enough.

It was bunk, all of it, and a fine man paid a harsh price for what some other proud men wanted to get done.

I can tell you I played more golf than Steve. He'd go out to NorthRiver Yacht Club and hit practice balls after work in the afternoon. He might have played two rounds a week, at the most, and I'm sure some of those were related to athletics department business.

It was a terrible injustice. If Steve had left the office to cut his yard three times a week, nobody would've said a word about it. But if he put a golf club in his hand, look out, the accusations started flying and some members of the news media made him look like a lazy slouch.

There has never been a better ambassador for the University of Alabama Athletics Department than Steve Sloan. There has never been a better person. There has never been a more loyal person.

It makes no difference to me what the alumni, the rumormongers and one school president said, Steve Sloan was a winner in every area.

Interestingly, as it worked out, the man hired to replace Steve was the athletics director when my time at Alabama came to an end in 1992. But my problems with him started long before that.

Please let me reset the stage for you, particularly to that time long before I was ousted as Alabama's basketball coach.

Also, let me do that by saying there isn't any doubt I made mistakes while coaching Alabama. I'll admit that. I'd give almost anything if some things that happened during my time in Tuscaloosa hadn't happened.

But, darn it, I didn't do the things I was accused of doing in newspapers and through other news media outlets — after what I perceived to be a feeding of the erroneous facts to the news media by sources within the athletics department.

It might be surprising to some of you to learn my problems with the athletics director who was there when I was let go started before he was appointed to the position, even as there was a lot of talk that he had the job locked up.

During the spring after Steve Sloan had resigned, or had been removed, I received a telephone call at home from Cecil "Hootie" Ingram, who was trying to become Alabama's athletics director. I had just come off the golf course at NorthRiver Yacht Club. I had already heard through the grapevine that Ingram didn't think I wanted him to be the athletics director.

I don't remember ever saying anything like that.

So I answered the telephone, Ingram identified himself and he said, "I understand you don't want me to be the athletics director at Alabama." I told him I had nothing to do with it, that I wasn't on the selection committee. Then he said, "Let me tell you something, if they name me athletics director, I'm not going to bother your program."

Blam. He hung up the telephone.

I couldn't believe it was happening. In fact, I went in and told Annette I had just received one of the stranger telephone calls of my life.

At that point, I had been named assistant athletics director for basketball, a position that allowed me to advance our sport while contributing to the good health of the University of Alabama Athletics Department. But listening to Ingram you would have thought I was there to take down the Crimson Tide.

Interestingly, talk about Ingram becoming the athletics director bothered people other than me. The most successful coach in our women's sports program came to me and voiced her concerns about him being appointed athletics directors. She said he had never advanced women's sports at any college he had worked, which included two in the Deep South.

But once Ingram was in place as athletics director, she reversed positions. Her entire approach to him seemed to change dramatically.

I found that humorous then. I find it humorous now.

From the day Ingram walked into that office as my boss, I

knew he wanted it to be curtains for me. I was not his man. It was obvious he was more comfortable in a setting where coaches working for him owed their jobs to his hire. I always thought his insecurity with me was based in large part on our basketball program being successful and profitable.

I knew it was going to be a rocky ride for me with Ingram in place as athletics director. It was that, for sure.

As for Bill Curry, the routinely criticized football coach, he didn't have a chance. Remember, he was hired by Dr. Joab Thomas, not Ingram. So it was just a matter of time until he was on his way to Kentucky from Alabama.

That type working relationship led to more problems than you can believe. To say it took some glimmer off the most successful period in the history of University of Alabama basketball would be a gross understatement.

When my problems developed, a harassment lawsuit filed by my secretary, Ingram told me I had his support. But it didn't take long for his position on the matter to appear contrary to that.

I had worked with three successful athletics directors — Paul Bryant, Ray Perkins and Steve Sloan — and now I was forced to fight a major battle with one who could not have cared less about my future. It was extremely obvious to virtually everybody in the athletics department that he was jealous of whatever public popularity I had, also the popularity of our basketball program that was thriving because of the efforts of some outstanding players and outstanding young men.

In summary, I'm sure Cecil "Hootie" Ingram received a great deal of enjoyment when I cleaned out my office and left Coleman Coliseum in 1992.

As for everything that has happened since then at the University of Alabama, well, I guess it's safe to say I'm as amazed as everybody else seems to be.

CHAPTER SEVEN

Football Coaches: I Liked Them All

Wimp Sanderson worked hard to make the University of Alabama basketball program as popular as possible

Although I've felt differently on a few occasions, the toughest job on the University of Alabama campus isn't coaching basketball. It's coaching football, by a long shot, and while in Tuscaloosa I saw four men fight long odds while serving the Crimson Tide.

They were Paul "Bear" Bryant, 1958 through 1982, Ray Perkins, 1983 through 1986, Bill Curry, 1987 through 1989, and Gene "Bebes" Stallings, 1990 through 1996, although I wasn't around for the last four years.

It was my privilege to work alongside those four men and I consider each a great person and a great coach. I like all four very much.

Obviously, because football is a way of life at Alabama, Coach Bryant, Coach Perkins, Coach Curry and Coach Stallings were extremely recognizable and, to varying degrees, each was the toast of the state at various times. Also, each had enormous power in the state and worked hard to make Crimson Tide football as good as it could be.

There were great times in football during my 32 years on campus, some average times and, on a few occasions, some bad times. But I noticed that as football went, enrollment in the university went, up and down, and that should tell you something about its importance. Also, the mood of the alumni went that way, at times spiraling out of control on both ends of the spectrum.

I thought football was important, too, and did all I could to be supportive of the coaches and the program. From time to time I would make telephone calls or visit with a prospect when he was on campus to help recruiting. I learned the importance of teamwork like that from Coach Bryant, who used to help our basketball program that way.

It's important, I think, for a basketball coach to understand the importance of Alabama football and where it should be at the national level. I was a good student of the sport. I knew its value and wasn't intimidated by it. After all, it was football money that enabled the athletics department to function.

Also, I was proud during the 1980s when we got the basketball program to a position where it could contribute huge sums of money to the athletics department. That hadn't been the case and, with the advent of more sports for women, it was an important financial boost.

I've said a lot about Coach Bryant, but I'd like to share a few more things that I thought made him such a fantastic leader. He was a genuine icon who arrived at Alabama after stops at Maryland, Kentucky and Texas A&M. A former Crimson Tide star end opposite Don Hutson, he returned to Tuscaloosa to rebuild football. It was a hard task because the program had managed only four wins and four ties during the previous three seasons.

Alabama was at the bottom. Coach Bryant brought us back and he was beloved and respected by fans and, in a lot of cases, opponents and their fans.

Coach Bryant knew strategy, excellent with Xs and Os, but was even better handling people. He surrounded himself with super assistant coaches because he had the ability to select winners.

A lot of those assistant coaches went on to become good head coaches. But some had a problem because they attempted to take on Coach Bryant's personality. I'm telling you that wasn't possible because there was only one Coach Bryant.

Actually, that's almost always true, no matter the teacher. I learned that in the early 1980s when I took over direction of the basketball program from C.M. Newton. I had to be myself, coach with my personality, not his, and sometimes coaches don't realize the importance of that.

Coach Bryant had what I think was a basic threefold plan for success. He controlled the state in recruiting players. He evaluated players, selected the right ones and put them in the right positions. He motivated his coaches to coach hard and his players to play hard.

Perhaps motivation was his strong suit, the big factor. Some played out of fear. Some played out of respect. Some played simply because they loved the game. But all of them wanted to please him and knew exactly what they had to do for the team to be successful.

Six national championships were the result of that.

Coach Bryant brought great distinction to the University of Alabama and the state. I see no reason to forget that great era for the Crimson Tide, although some people think the past is gone and should be put aside. In other words, I firmly believe we can learn a lot by studying the characteristics of a great leader like him and, in some manner, become better people.

The same is true with Coach Ralph "Shug" Jordan, who coached Auburn for a quarter of a century. The competition he and Coach Bryant had during the late 1950s, the 1960s and half of the 1970s provided sports fans with a great deal of entertainment. The alums and players fought hard, too, at times to the point of resentment, but that all went together to make one of the best rivalries in the nation. Like in any sport, the fierce competition was healthy.

Coach Bryant taught character. He had players with loads of it. Many have gone on to become successful men in their professions. A classic example is Mal Moore, the current athletics director at Alabama. He was a super offensive coordinator, too.

In an effort to restore national prominence in football, Coach

Bryant controlled everything, as he needed to. He even took some basketball scholarships and gave them to football players, which was legal during that time when there were no limits on the number of players. He found innovative ways to use playing rules, often forcing the NCAA to change some. He covered every angle, like a master, and the success was bewildering.

One of the finest attributes Coach Bryant had was the ability to change with the times. He knew defense and kicking were the ways to win in the early 1960s. He knew passing was becoming more important in the late 1960s and 1970s. He knew the trends and stayed on top of them, often coming up with some of his own.

Who can forget what he did in 1971, when Alabama went to the wishbone offense.

The program was down, having lost 10 games in two seasons, 1969 and 1970, and some people thought Coach Bryant was finished. But after playing against Oklahoma, which ran the wishbone offense, in the 1970 Astro-Bluebonnet Bowl, a 24-24 tie, and conferring with his friend Coach Darrell Royal of Texas, he decided to utilize that formation. Under a shroud of secrecy, Alabama put in the wishbone formation during preseason practice and sprung it on Southern Cal in Los Angeles on September 10, 1971. The Crimson Tide won, 17-10, and went on to an 11-1 record.

The man people were saying was over the hill led Alabama to 103 wins during the 1970s and in 1981 became the winningest college coach in history.

When Coach Bryant retired in 1982, there was a lot of speculation about who the next coach would be. Howard Schnellenberger was mentioned. I think "Bebes" Stallings was interviewed, although he had a long contract in place with the Dallas Cowboys. Nobody really knew which way Alabama would turn at that important time.

Ray Perkins was coaching the New York Giants of the National Football League. He telephoned Dr. Gaylon McCollough, a former Alabama center and an influential member of the alumni, and told him he was interested in becoming the Crimson Tide coach.

The hiring of Ray Perkins, a super pass receiver for Alabama during the 1960s, was done quietly and took a little longer than most people realize. Coach Bryant was extremely sick during the 1982 season and he knew it would be his last. So the wheels were turning for a few months before an announcement was made.

If Coach Bryant had been doing the hiring, which he wasn't, I'm not sure Ray would have been his choice. I think he was leaning toward "Bebes" Stallings. But I do know that at some point a few weeks before the announcement was made Coach Bryant was in New York seated beside Ray at a dinner party. He leaned toward him and said, "Walter, it's time to come home."

Walter Ray Perkins did return to Alabama and faced what I'd term an almost impossible task following a legend. Almost everything he did from the outset came under constant scrutiny and the national news media was all over the story.

As I stated earlier while talking about him as an athletics director, a good one, Ray stepped on a lot of toes while making changes. One of the first things he did was take down the observation tower Coach Bryant had used during practice sessions on Thomas Field. That was like destroying a monument among Alabama fans, or defacing the Washington Monument, to continue a previous thought.

I admit I cringed a little when the tower came down, but I understood what Ray was thinking. He wanted to be closer to his players during practice, on the field with them. He just didn't think about the backlash.

Regardless of those shortcomings and painful moments for

Ray Perkins, he worked as hard as any Alabama coach in history. He was relentless in his pursuit. His records, 8-4, 5-6, 9-2-1 and 10-3, were not earth shattering, not when compared to Coach Bryant's, but to me it looked like the Crimson Tide was on the verge of making an impact nationally when he left.

Ray had most of the Alabama Family together when he departed for Tampa Bay. There are some people who think he jumped ship, so to speak, took the pro football money and ran. That's not exactly true. He was asking the administration for some assurances he thought were necessary to keep the Crimson Tide moving forward and he wasn't satisfied with the answers he received. Also, there were some big boosters who were sitting more squarely on their wallets and he saw that as a troublesome sign because those at Tennessee, Florida, Georgia and Auburn were contributing mightily.

So Ray was gone, sadly for me, and Bill Curry was in place as coach. Thus started one of the more troubling times in the history of the program.

Simply put, Bill was never accepted because he wasn't an Alabama man.

As early as the day Bill was named coach, shots started flying in several directions and did until he left after the 1989 season. The main targets were Dr. Joab Thomas, the school president who hired him, Steve Sloan, the athletics director who had nothing to do with the hiring, and, of course, Bill himself.

People were disgruntled for a variety of reasons.

Bill had been unable to beat Auburn and Coach Pat Dye while at Georgia Tech. Obviously, that's important to Alabama fans, as well as me.

Most people thought a man with Alabama ties was more suited for the position. Adding fuel to that, Bill arrived from Georgia Tech, a bitter rival for the Crimson Tide in the past. He had played under Bobby Dodd, a rival for Coach Bryant. Fans with good memories recalled the Darwin Holt and Chick Granning brutality issue from the early 1960s and Coach Bryant having to wear a helmet on the sidelines at a game in Atlanta because the Yellow Jackets' fans were throwing whiskey bottles at him and his players.

Several people simply didn't think Bill looked like an Alabama coach. They remembered Coach Bryant looking as if he was bleeding on the sideline while trying to help his teams win. They remembered Ray Perkins casting a cold glare at officials during games. In Bill Curry they saw a man who in their minds was a whole lot different, a guy from Georgia Tech wearing a sweater with "Alabama" written across its front.

Dr. Thomas didn't help Bill with a remark he made after hiring him. He said he wanted a man with integrity and he no longer wanted the University of Alabama to be considered just a football factory. A lot of people never understood what he meant by that.

After all that happened, whether fairly or unfairly, I can't say for sure that Bill Curry was the right man for the job. But I can say he was a gentleman, he had good success, 7-5, 9-3 and 10-2 records, and I liked him and counted him among my friends.

Bill was ridiculed by the alumni and the news media and I think he handled it. He was tough, a nice man with a great family. Steve Sloan, the athletics director, supported him like a rock, as he should have. Some of the assistant athletics directors, who know who they are, and some of his assistant coaches, who know who they are, weren't so loyal.

Any way you cut it, Bill took Alabama to three bowl games and won the Southeastern Conference championship in 1989. No, he never beat Auburn, losing 10-0, 13-10 and 30-20, and the last loss came at Jordan-Hare Stadium, which added to the sour tastes in the mouths of a lot of foolish so called supporters.

When the new athletics director came on the scene, the same one with whom I had so much trouble, he had to deal with the Bill

Curry situation. He designed a contract for the coach that wasn't very good, to say the least, and provided all manner of ways he could be fired.

As this was unfolding, C.M. Newton, the athletics director at Kentucky, expressed an interest in Bill moving to that program. He was more impressed than the Alabama people seemed to be.

C.M. came down to visit with Bill and Carolyn Curry, people Annette and I really liked. So I went over to his house to visit with C.M. and them. We had a nice visit and I left thinking it was probably in Bill's best interest to take the Kentucky job and leave his troubles at Alabama behind. Of course, he did that.

So, suddenly, Alabama football seemed to be starting over again as our basketball program was a starting a run of three consecutive NCAA Tournament berths.

The search for a new coach was fairly short.

Richard Williamson was a name often heard. He had been a Crimson Tide player, a split end during the 1960s, and had experienced some success at Memphis State. He had a great football mind, no doubt about it, and he called me during that time to solicit support. I thought he was a fine candidate. I think the higher up powers thought he might not have had enough glamorous success, that the program needed a coach with a stronger name.

So a trip was arranged to Paris, Texas to talk to Gene "Bebes" Stallings, who got the job and by the hardest restored Alabama to its rightful place among the elite programs in the nation.

As I said earlier, I met "Bebes" when he was a brash and young assistant coach in the early 1960s. In fact, if you'll recall, Annette and I moved into a house Gene and Ruth Ann vacated in Abrams Place.

"Bebes" was impressive back then. He handled the defensive secondary for Coach Bryant and did a great job. He had a winning personality among supporters and was a great speaker.

He was a little harder to get to know on a one on one basis because he was so aggressive in his approach to football. He was so consumed by the sport he used the off season to help Coach Bryant write a short little book about what it takes to win.

In the mid-1960s, or thereabout, "Bebes" left Alabama and went to Texas A&M, where he had played under Coach Bryant. It didn't work out for him there like he had hoped, but he did have an extremely memorable victory over Alabama, 20-16, in the 1968 Cotton Bowl. He owns one of only five victories Coach Bryant's former assistant coaches scored over him.

Most people know about "Bebes" coaching under Tom Landry with the Dallas Cowboys, then as head coach for Phoenix of the NFL. He had the credentials, had been around the block, and that's what Alabama wanted.

"Bebes" got off to a terrible start at Alabama. He lost his first three games, to Southern Miss, Florida and Georgia, but none by more than four points. There were rivals ridiculing the program and, to be truthful, some Crimson Tide fans were more than a little concerned.

But the record that season was 7-5, including a win over Auburn, the first of three in a row, the record in 1991 was 11-1 and the record in 1992 was 13-0 and resulted in the first national championship for Alabama since 1979. His final record with the Crimson Tide was 70-16-1, not counting the bevy of victories that came during his years as an assistant coach in Tuscaloosa.

"Bebes" did it with an old school approach, run first and pass if you have to, and a lot of people didn't like that. Coach Steve Spurrier was passing like crazy at Florida and winning that way and a huge chunk of Alabama fans wanted Stallings to open up his offensive attack.

I couldn't believe fans weren't satisfied with simply winning, rather wanted Alabama to win a certain way. But that's about the size of it and when I left in 1992 there was a big faction of the alumni that still hadn't accepted "Bebes" the way he should have been welcomed. It was winning football, pure and simple, and should have been applauded. However, like I said, it's a tough job and it's difficult to please everybody.

Meanwhile, "Bebes" and Ruth Ann and Annette and I rekindled a friendship that had started in 1960 when we attended the same church. We got closer this time and enjoyed the association.

Like a lot of people, I've secured a lot of tremendous inspiration from John Mark Stallings, their son who was a Down's Syndrome child at birth. He was born at about the same time our second son, Scott, was born and it was little difficult for "Bebes" to accept at that time.

But, gee, you talk about an inseparable pair, "Bebes" and John Mark, and the book Gene wrote about their experiences together is a wonderful read. They have a great family, simply put, including a fantastic husband and wife team, a terrific son and super daughters.

On a humorous note, "Bebes" and I used to get a kick out of John Mark mimicking my sideline behavior during games. His impersonations were pretty good, too, all the way down to the squirming and the scowling.

Gene weathered the Antonio Langham mess with class and kept winning. While there was still a lagging sector of so called supporters who didn't approve of his coaching style, I think it's safe to say his place in the history of Alabama football is secure.

I'm not sure of everything that happened to cause "Bebes" to resign after the 1996 season. But I've heard enough to know he didn't see eye to eye with a new athletics director, who has since been replaced, and a new president, who as of this writing is still on the scene.

I'll always admire "Bebes" for walking away quietly, leaving with dignity and immediately putting his energies into spending more time with Ruth Ann, John Mark, the daughters and the remainder of his family.

Hey, that all sounds familiar to me — success, problems with leadership, departure and, of course, good times with family members as we recall many of the great times in basketball that I'm about to share with you.

CHAPTER EIGHT

The 1980s: A Decade to Remember

(Continued)

The 1980s found the Crimson Tide becoming a dominating force in the Southeastern Conference Tournament

To me it sounded like somebody was trying to jinx us, but late in the 1980s people in the news media started referring to the Southeastern Conference Tournament as the University of Alabama Invitational. It was a compliment, of course, the result of us having made it to finals of the event nine times in the dozen years I was directing the Crimson Tide basketball program.

Being humble is one thing. Being deceitful is another. So I won't try to minimize that accomplishment because any knowledgeable fan knows how tough the SEC has been for three decades. Anyway, we made the finals in 1982, 1983, 1985, 1986, 1987, 1989, 1990, 1991 and 1992 and we won the championship five times.

Making the NCAA Tournament field 10 times and advancing to the Sweet 16 six times is something else my players, my assistant coaches and I are proud about. From a personal standpoint, I'm more disappointed I couldn't take Alabama to the Elite Eight or Final Four. However, being three wins away from a national championship game is hard to do and I'll cherish the years we got that far.

I'll save a few special memories of the SEC Tournament and the NCAA Tournament for a later chapter or two. But I can't help sending a few your way in this one.

We got a major SEC Tournament victory in 1982, my second season, and it was a crowning accomplishment for what I believe was a terrific team. That came on a dramatic evening at Rupp Arena in Lexington, Kentucky, when we beat the Kentucky Wildcats, 48-46, in the championship game.

Our record that season was 24-7, 12-6 in the SEC regular

season, and we made it to the second round of the NCAA Tournament. We beat St. John's, 69-68, in Uniondale, New York and got eliminated by North Carolina, 74-69, in Raleigh, N.C. That's not an easy draw to handle, facing two teams in their home states with a possible run at a national championship at stake. Also, James Worthy and Michael Jordan played for NC.

I've already talked about a lot of the players we put on the floor in 1982 because all of them except Ken Johnson were a part of our 1981 team. But there was a great addition in Ennis Whatley, a freshman guard who along with Mike Davis and Eric Richardson gave us a powerful punch at that position, and a great addition in Bobby Lee Hurt, a freshman center.

In fact, Mike had tremendous versatility as a guard. He was a player who always gave great effort, to the point of fatigue. He was a smart player who had studied basketball for a long time.

Eddie Phillips, who is second on the school scoring list behind Reggie King, showed more maturity, although I don't think he was ever sold on me. He led us in scoring with 15.5 points per game and in rebounding with 8.6 per game. But that was a team with great balance and gone were the secret meetings that had hurt us a year earlier.

We had three horrible games that season, a loss at Tennessee after we won our first nine, a loss at Kentucky and a loss at Vanderbilt on the final evening of the regular season. That last loss cost us a share of the SEC championship.

Also, we had a terrible tailspin during the final third of the regular season in which we lost three conference games in a row — at Ole Miss, at LSU and to Kentucky in Memorial Coliseum.

Anybody who watched us in our final regular season game in Nashville, when Vanderbilt demolished us, 80-63, saw one of the worst performances I can remember. The Commodores went back door on us about two dozen times for layups and we shot like the basket was about four inches wide. The reaction was pretty gruesome: Alabama isn't playing good enough to do anything in the SEC Tournament.

I knew something other people didn't. There isn't any reason to go into it in detail, so let's just say a few of our players didn't have their minds on basketball when they went on the court in Nashville. I found out later from a manager that some of our guys broke team rules on the afternoon before Vanderbilt crushed us. You talk about a coach on the prowl, so mad I could have spit, that was me when I learned that happened on a day when we could have earned a share of the SEC championship.

We beat Vanderbilt, 79-68, in Tuscaloosa. We got beat by Vanderbilt, 80-63, in Nashville. You figure that out, especially since we were a lot better team going down the stretch than we were early in the season.

I had my players' attention when we went to Lexington for the SEC Tournament. We got past Georgia in the first round and Tennessee in the second round. Then we caught Kentucky, which had a 22-7 record, in the championship game.

There wasn't a shot clock then, so we played as deliberately as we could. Ennis Whatley, Mike Davis and Eric Richardson were superb handling the basketball. The fans might not have appreciated the low scoring, but I sure did when the game was knotted at 46 in the final minute.

Kentucky had the basketball and came across midcourt. Paul Galvan, an excellent official for several years, called a walking violation on them and we had possession with a chance to win.

I called a timeout and told our players I wanted to clear the right side of the court, put the ball in Ennis' hands and let him take it to the basket to shoot or get fouled. It worked just right, only Ennis missed the shot. The ball popped up and out into the lane, Eddie Phillips rebounded it and put it in the basket.

We led 48-46 with a few seconds remaining. Kentucky got the basketball to Melvin Turpin, their big center, and he missed a fairly short shot at the buzzer.

Without question, it was a classic victory for Alabama. I was elated and excited. So was Dr. Joab Thomas, our school president. I saw him with a grin on his face as Big Al, our elephant mascot, carried him to midcourt to celebrate with our players, managers and cheerleaders.

The next game, the victory over St. John's, was a big one, too. In fact, Ray Perkins, who was coaching the New York Giants at the time, came by our dressing room after the win, which was a thrill for our players and me.

Then came a game I'll remember until I die, the loss to North Carolina on North Carolina State's home court.

Tell me if any of these North Carolina starters sound familiar: Matt Doherty, James Worthy, Sam Perkins, Jimmy Black and Michael Jordan. Oh, so you have never heard of Jimmy Black?

That's the task we faced that night in Raleigh.

We were assigned the North Carolina State bench for the game. But Coach Dean Smith and his Tar Heels beat us to it, I suppose to get a psychological advantage.

The gymnasium didn't have great lights and CBS Sports came in and installed a new set. I was wearing a suede sport coat, plain and not plaid, and I wasn't smart enough to take it off because it was the hottest game I've ever been around. I was drenched when it was over. The sport coat went in the garbage can because there was no way to clean out all of the sweat.

It was a heck of a game and we had a great chance to win it. That made the loss more painful and it took me a long time to get over it, especially when I looked at film of it. I don't want to take anything away from North Carolina, which became national champion, but we could have gotten a victory that night.

It was interesting one of the officials who worked our game that night also worked one we had played against Southern Cal when C.M. Newton was coach at Alabama. He called five technicals on us then. He blew his whistle a lot in Raleigh.

We held Worthy to 16 points, Perkins to 15 points and Jordan to 11 points and lost to the eventual national champion.

Our record in 1983 was 20-12 and it wasn't that good in the SEC, 8-10, a tie for eighth place. As you might surmise, we struggled, we spurted and we struggled. It was a rare occurrence when we got knocked out of the conference tournament in the first round, but that was the case that year.

I've looked back at that and tried to figure out what went wrong and I still draw a blank. The only thing I can see is we lacked a dominating inside player. We had great guards, maybe too many. Plus, Bobby Lee Hurt, as a sophomore, and Buck Johnson, as a freshman, simply weren't ready to go to war inside against larger and more seasoned players.

Adding to my perplexity, that was a team that defeated a fine Southern Cal team, 74-61, and a Patrick Ewing-led Georgetown team, 94-73, in a December tournament in Los Angeles and defeated UCLA in Pauley Pavilion on the day Coach Paul "Bear" Bryant was buried.

Had it not been for those three wins it would have been a forgettable year, other than the fact ol' Wimp just can't put aside losses.

There are a lot of coaches, make that most of them, who would toot a trumpet if they accomplished 20 wins in a season. But I wasn't like that, not when a team had 12 losses and, in my opinion, didn't tap its potential.

In fairness to the 1983 Alabama team, we had a lot of injuries and we had a lot of young players.

Also, we were recruiting some powerhouse talent that would put us near the top of the universe before those players were finished in Tuscaloosa.

Now that I've belabored my disappointment, let me say the victory over Georgetown might have been the best performance by an Alabama team during my tenure. "Enimo" Whatley and The Gang put on quite a show and we were running away from Coach John Thompson's Hoyas when time expired.

The victory over UCLA was a killer. We were ahead by one point when one of their players who might have been confused by the score fouled Mike Davis. He had two free throws. The first one hit the front of the rim, bounded against the backboard and went in. The next one was a swish and we had a memorable victory over the Number 1 team in the nation.

We started Mark Farmer, a 6-foot-11 center from Arab, Alabama against UCLA. He wasn't what you'd call a superstar, but he stepped up that night and played extremely well. I remember I congratulated him after the game for a fine effort and told him he should be proud because both television sets in Arab were on that night.

We beat Auburn, 86-78, in Tuscaloosa in the final regular season game. Their coach was one of my dear friends in the profession, Sonny Smith, and, lo and behold, we drew them again in the first round of the SEC Tournament.

Sonny knows me like a book, which I'll talk about later when addressing characters in the SEC, and he had Auburn ready in the tournament. We got past the Tigers, 62-61, then beat Kentucky and Mississippi State to advance to the title game against Georgia.

At last, I thought, these guys are starting to play like I had anticipated they would all season.

Little did I know, Georgia whipped us, 86-71, which is as much a flogging as a whipping. But in our defense, that was an interesting Georgia team that went on to the Final Four in Albuquerque, New Mexico. We had been beaten, but not by a slouch.

I walked off the court that afternoon at the Birmingham-

Jefferson Civic Center and heard a public address announcement that Alabama would play Lamar in the first round of the NCAA Tournament. I was ecstatic. A team that had experienced highs and lows had made it to the Big Show because we had played a lot of nonconference powers and had done well.

In a departure from the norm, I greeted sports writers and sports broadcasters at our dressing room door and invited them inside. Once there, I congratulated our players for making it to the SEC Tournament finals and announced we would be playing Lamar in the NCAA Tournament in Houston, Texas.

Well, Bobby Lee Hurt, who happens to be one of the more personable guys in Alabama basketball history, quickly said, "Lamar? Who is that?"

The news media heard that remark and had its bait, a huge chunk of steak, and sports writers and sports broadcasters sent those words into print and across the airways — "Lamar? Who is that?"

We found out in a major way. Lamar beat us, 73-50, really killed us, and I think that might have been the most disappointing game I had at Alabama, at least from an effort standpoint. We never seemed to get into a rhythm. I don't think I had our players motivated. We had some off the floor problems that might have taken a toll on us, things that'll remain private.

The 20-12 record we had in 1983 wasn't up to high Alabama standards. But it looked darn fine after the war our 1984 team fought to bring home an 18-12 record.

Frankly, I saw some slippage in our demeanor. But I felt fine about our recruiting efforts, with Jim Farmer and Terry Coner, two fine shooters and playmakers, on board and Derrick McKey and Mark Gottfried acting as if they were interested in joining the Crimson Tide.

It was at about that time I felt much more comfortable with my position as head coach and I was convinced we could compete game in and game out in the Southeastern Conference.

Our fans were starting to accept me more as coach. They definitely liked the way our players performed, as they should have because they really worked at it.

All of us ached through the 1984 season, from a 1-3 start in the SEC regular season to a loss to Illinois State in the first round of the NCAA Tournament in Lincoln, Nebraska. Of course, Ennis Whatley decided to turn pro after his sophomore season, 1983, and I'm sure we would've been much stronger with him than we were without him. He was an impact player from the start.

The SEC Tournament was tough, too, at least by our growing standards. We went an overtime to beat LSU in the first round, 72-70, and lost to a fine Kentucky team in the second round, 48-46, the same darn score we had when we beat them in 1982.

Illinois State eliminated us from the NCAA Tournament on the last shot. We had a one point lead, 48-47, and I called a timeout to change defenses. They nailed one at the buzzer to beat us by a point.

It was one of the more even games I've seen. It was physical, but both teams shot only two free throws. We made both of ours and they made one. We were even in field goals at 23 until they made the last one.

That loss doesn't stick out much in the minds of most Alabama fans. But I consider it one of the three or four more disappointing losses in my 12 years.

We bounced back in 1985 and posted a 23-10 record. It was an outstanding year because seven of our losses were by four points or fewer.

I was getting concerned about Auburn again because my buddy Sonny Smith was getting some great talent and challenging our superiority in the state. They had beaten us twice in 1984 and we had two wicked games with them during the 1985 regular season. We won 60-55 on their court and

74-72 in two overtimes on our court.

I've always thought you've got to win your state before you can think about winning the SEC, so those margins of victory were a concern.

Meanwhile, Sonny was fighting many of the same things C.M. Newton, John Bostick and I had dealt with in the 1970s. His fans base was not much and he had little support from his athletics department leadership. Pat Dye had the Auburn football program on a roll and interest in basketball was at an ebb.

It was taking a heavy toll on Sonny, who wasn't feeling good at the time, and he was ready to walk away from it all. I know it's strange to hear this from a competitive guy, but I really felt for him and I didn't want to jump off of a cliff when his team beat my team in the finals of the SEC Tournament.

We had the easier path to the finals because Auburn had to play in the first round while we had a bye. We beat Mississippi State, 42-31, when they tried to slow the pace on our racehorses, and we beat Georgia, 74-53, in the semifinals. Meanwhile, Auburn won three times in three days to get to the championship game.

We led at Birmingham-Jefferson Civic Center for almost the entire game, but we couldn't run off and leave Auburn. They caught us at the end of regulation and beat us in overtime, 53-49. I looked pretty ragged after that game. However, I must say Sonny put on a coaching clinic in that tournament, skillfully getting a fatigued team through four hard games.

But Alabama wasn't finished after the SEC Tournament because we received a berth in the NCAA Tournament and made a good run.

We beat Arizona in the first round, 50-41, in Albuquerque, New Mexico. That team was coached by Lute Olsen, who has had a lot of success with that program.

The trip was fantastic. It was a great atmosphere. Arizona had a lot of fans there, with that being a neighboring state, and they were all dressed in red, white and blue. They wore caps that had an "A" on them. They waved a big flag with an "A" on it. They were a highly spirited bunch.

I tried to take an edge off of that advantage by convincing my players all of those folks were wearing an "A" that stood for Alabama, that our fans had flocked to New Mexico to support them. I don't think I had many takers on that one. Still, we played a great basketball game and beat them.

The box score from that game features some names that are familiar to Crimson Tide fans who saw us getting on a roll. Bobby Lee Hurt, then a veteran, led us in scoring with 14 points. Buck Johnson, then a veteran, scored 12. Terry Coner, a sophomore guard who would become a classic playmaker for us, scored 10, Jim Farmer scored eight and Mark Gottfried scored four.

But guess who the CBS Sports player of the game was that night?

The honoree was Derrick McKey, a freshman, who didn't score a point but earned player of the game distinction because of his defense, his ability to block shots and his rebounding. I think that's probably the only time a player of the game in the NCAA Tournament was a guy who didn't scratch in the scoring book. Of course, anybody who saw "Big D" play for us understands the numerous ways he could make his presence known.

Bobby Lee Hurt seemed to carry us through our next NCAA Tournament game, a 63-59 victory over Coach J.D. Barnette's Virginia Commonwealth team. He scored 19 points and had 13 rebounds. He played from pillar to post, all 40 minutes.

Buck Johnson got 10 rebounds for us against VCU and we left Albuquerque on a high, in the Sweet Sixteen.

By the way, an assistant coach at VCU that year was David Hobbs, who became my longtime assistant coach and my replacement at Alabama.

I can't think about that trip and those wins over Arizona and

VCU without remembering how delighted my friend Harry Cole was with our success. My little short buddy with a bald head and big smile, a Tuscaloosa real estate executive, was grinning from ear to ear. He looked like he had swallowed a funny bar.

Harry was my golfing buddy, gin rummy buddy and confidant. Bless his soul, he has passed away and I miss seeing him almost every day. I can still envision him sitting on our team bus after games in places like Athens, Georgia, Oxford, Mississippi and Baton Rouge, Louisiana because he was almost always there to support us, at times the only traveling Crimson Tide fan in the stands.

I'm sure Harry was with me the night before our victory over Virginia Commonwealth and I guess I'll forgive him for letting me eat too much Mexican food. Anyway, I've never been as sick in my life for a game. I had to stretch out on the training table in the dressing room as our team warmed up, trying for relief, and it was touch and go on the bench for both halves.

Obviously, a victory was good medicine for me as we moved toward Denver, Colorado and a third round game against North Carolina State.

Kentucky and St. John's were in Denver, too, and I recall not much was written or said about Alabama being in the tournament. It was like the news media didn't think we belonged in the Sweet Sixteen.

That's also the year Joe Hall resigned as Kentucky's coach after his team lost to St. John's. He's the former assistant coach under Adolph Rupp who led the Wildcats to a 297-100 record between 1973 and 1985. In many ways our careers ran parallel because he waited a long time to get his chance and he did well after getting the opportunity to lead that prestigious program 13 seasons.

Our game with N.C. State was nip and tuck all the way. It went back and forth. They had Anthony "Spud" Webb, a pint sized guard, and Lorenzo Charles, a fine forward. Their coach was Jim Volvano, a good one who later died after a gallant fight against cancer.

N.C. State beat us, 61-56, in a remarkably hardfought game. I really felt bad for our players after that loss because they played terrific defense and shot field goals good, too. As it worked out, it was another loss in the Sweet Sixteen and I left the court that night thinking we had come mighty close to the Elite Eight.

But that was an almost there season, another one, and that game against North Carolina State was sort of a coming out party for Terry Coner. He scored 18 points, a strong performance for a sophomore, and with sophomore Jim Farmer and freshman Derek McKey rounding into form, I felt extremely good about the future of the program.

After I take a break to tell a few humorous and mischievous recruiting stories and to talk about some memorable coaches and other characters, you'll learn more about the 1980s, a decade to remember in the history of Alabama basketball.

CHAPTER NINE

Recruiting: Wild and Funny Stories

Part I

Reggie King, twice SEC Player of the Year during the 1970s, was a prize recruit for the University of Alabama basketball program

If you want to eat a lot of fried chicken and home baked cake, hear a lot of lies and spend a lot of restless nights with a nervous stomach, try recruiting high school basketball players for a college program.

You'll get that and much more.

Recruiting is the lifeblood of a basketball program because without good players good coaches will be losers and soon unemployed.

Recruiting is followed by the masses, about like gas prices and the weather, and most fans know when a coach has failed to get a prospect he badly needs and badly covets.

Recruiting is an opportunity to brush shoulders with numerous people with whom you have absolutely nothing in common, outside of the basketball player being courted.

Recruiting is important. No, change that statement to recruiting is I-M-P-O-R-T-A-N-T, which is why a coach better do it right and have his share of success.

I've been down that road, as well as a bunch out in the country and a bunch on city streets, so I'll tell you a few stories about the recruitment of players who were keys to the success we had at Alabama during the 1970s, 1980s and part of the 1990s.

Let me begin with the spring after my first year as Alabama's head coach, the 1981 recruiting season, because there's no way I can adequately tell you how important it was for us to sign Bobby Lee Hurt and Ennis Whatley, the best two players in the state. Then I'll scattershoot, giving you a dose of things seen and things heard while making a few comments about the players and what they meant to me personally and to the Crimson Tide.

I don't know of a recruiting story more unique than our recruitment of Bobby Lee Hurt, a happy go lucky guy out of Butler High School in Huntsville, Alabama. He played under me from 1982 through 1985 and made major contributions. A 6-foot-9 forward and center, he played on teams that posted an 85-41 record and played in four NCAA Tournaments. He had between 41 and 51 blocked shots every season, an impressive total. He was an absolute joy to coach.

As a high school player and a college player, Bobby Lee never met a person he didn't like, nor one he would ever tell no. He was a fine person, a personable guy with a grin as wide as the Atlantic Ocean, and was a showman who genuinely enjoyed the attention he received as a high school recruit. To give you an example of his flamboyance, he loved disco music, or rap, and he served as guest disc jockey for a Tuscaloosa radio station while he played for us.

I spent a ton of time recruiting Bobby Lee and as the months passed I wasn't sure we'd get him. Hawaii, of all places, came into play in a major way. In fact, that was our biggest rival in his recruitment because he had grandiose ideas about the islands setting. Late in the game, Maryland came hard, with Coach "Lefty" Driesell making a strong push.

I went to Huntsville and stayed a week at a Holiday Inn. Newspaper reporters were all over the place and they stayed on our heels. So one day I took Bobby Lee to an accountant's office to get away from the crowd. We bought a big bucket of chicken at about noon and I kept him in there until dusk. I made a hard sales pitch, told him how good our program was and how good it would be if he was in our lineup. When our visit ended, he got up and said, "Coach Sanderson, I'm still going to Hawaii."

At that point, I made a harder sales pitch. People have said I got down on both knees and begged Bobby Lee to come to Alabama. That's not true. I only got down on one knee.

We had an interesting problem with Hawaii. Gomer Pyle from the Andy Griffith television show, or Jim Nabors by formal name, was a Sylacauga, Alabama native and an Alabama graduate living in Hawaii. He had befriended people at the school and had guaranteed Bobby Lee a job cutting sugar cane for eight bucks an hour. That was a lot of money then and seemed to be the decisive thing in the recruiting process. I doubt Gomer Pyle followed basketball, but he was playing a strong role.

I was trying to get to Gomer Pyle to tell him his alma mater was recruiting Bobby Lee and he was killing us. I knew he wouldn't listen to me, so I attempted to get Coach Paul "Bear" Bryant involved.

After hearing what was going on, Coach Bryant agreed we needed to get in touch with Gomer and get this thing stopped. Unfortunately, Gomer was on a ship in Australia. Ultimately, we got what we called a shore to ship message from Coach Bryant to Gomer in which he told him to back off, please, that he was hurting Alabama by helping Hawaii.

Then "Lefty" came charging on behalf of Maryland. He was a dynamic recruiter, a funny man, the type guy Bobby Lee would like a lot and probably did.

But after a couple more weeks it came down to Alabama and Hawaii and, finally, Jerry Rice, Bobby Lee's terrific coach at Butler High School, called a meeting to get the process completed. He sat me down with the coach from Hawaii on Friday afternoon and said, "Okay, enough is enough. Bobby Lee has gone through two years of this. He needs 48 hours to think about what he wants to do. At some point Monday, he'll come in here and announce his decision. I don't want anybody to contact Bobby Lee by telephone or in person this entire weekend."

I felt like Jerry Rice sort of favored us over Hawaii and had an idea what was going on. So I crossed my fingers and agreed we wouldn't contact him. The Hawaii coach did, too, and he must have had his fingers crossed.

I was thinking hard when I left that meeting. I knew if I didn't get Bobby Lee Hurt and Ennis Whatley while going into my second season as Alabama's coach that I could fold my tent and go to the house.

So as soon as I got my car cranked, off to Bobby Lee's house I went. It wasn't long before I was visiting again with Bobby Lee and his family, making our sales pitch.

I learned about a year ago from Riley Wallace, the assistant coach at Hawaii, that he and the head coach were at their hotel when a light went off in his head. They jumped in their car, drove to Bobby Lee's house and found my state car parked there.

Finally, we were able to get Bobby Lee, in large part because of Cotton Johnson, who Bobby Lee worked for in Huntsville. He was extremely close to Bobby Lee and he loved Alabama sports. His son, by the way, is Hoss Johnson, who played football for the Crimson Tide.

It was a bizarre experience, to say the least. We spent what seemed like endless hours trying to get Bobby Lee. He spent endless hours saying yes, then maybe and then no to everybody who called him.

In fact, there was one time in the process when he told the folks from Hawaii he was going to Alabama. They left for home. When they got to either Los Angeles or San Francisco, they called Bobby Lee one more time from the airport. He told them he had changed his mind, that he might want to go to Hawaii. They got on a plane, returned to Huntsville and still couldn't sign him.

That recruitment created an uproar in the state that even had the news media at odds. Some of the news media seemed to paint a negative picture of our program in an effort to help UAB establish its program. Some of the news media came to our defense. One of the ridiculous stories said we bought Bobby Lee Hurt with money funneled through Cotton Johnson. The most ridiculous line of thought was that Bobby Lee pocketed money he collected from soft drink machines.

As time passed, the stories seemed to become more outrageous. I tried to ignore them and keep recruiting.

Cotton Johnson, a good man, got dragged through the mud in an unfair and brutal manner by news media members who had agendas guiding them.

Ultimately, the NCAA had some investigators look into the matter. They were thorough with their search. They talked to a lot of people. They found nothing.

Now, let's look at the recruitment of Ennis Whatley, which was unusual, too, but for a different reason.

The Ennis Whatley recruitment is the only time I've seen when the prospect didn't show up for our official visit with him and his family.

Leroy McClendon was an assistant coach with us at that time and he and I went to Birmingham for the visit. We talked with Ennis' wonderful mother, made our sales pitch, and talked briefly with his father.

As we were leaving, I said, "Leroy, how in the world can we sign a prospect when he won't come to the official visit with us?"

Leroy smiled and said, "We'll manage some way."

Ennis had committed to UAB. Ennis had talked to Auburn. Everybody in the nation was in there because he was that kind of player, a superstar, a 6-foot-3 guard who could dribble, pass, shoot and play defense. He was good enough to turn pro after his sophomore season, 1983, and I was proud for him but extremely disappointed to lose him after such a short time.

Eventually, we got Ennis signed and I was tickled pink. I had the two I had to get.

Now I'll take you back a long way, to the 1970s, when we

started getting players from our state left and right. It was dynamic time for high school basketball in our state and recruiting was tough on the one hand because a lot of out of state programs came calling and easy on the one hand because of the abundance of talent.

T.R. Dunn was a special player at West End High School in Birmingham. I worked several years on him, watched him play what seems like a hundred games, and really went at it hard in 1974, when he signed with us and played as a freshman. He was 6-foot-4, perfectly built, and he could play guard and forward.

T.R. was quietly mannered, unselfish and a good student. He had a marvelous mother who had raised him right. But he was the hardest guy in the world to get a commitment from.

A high school coach in Birmingham created a headache for me during the recruiting process. He went to a basketball clinic in New York, ran into Dean Smith, the North Carolina coach, and told him about T.R. Dunn, a super player and extremely polite person. So they came in and made a hard run on him.

In those years we could spend as much time with a prospect as we wanted. We could camp in the back yard, take the family out for every meal and go for long drives every day, if we wanted to do those things. It was wide open recruiting, although buying players was as illegal then as it is now.

I had a couple of alums in Birmingham who were a great deal of help. Frank Nix, who played for me at Carbon Hill and was later killed in an airplane crash, was influential in the T.R. Dunn recruitment. He got his dad a job and I think he stayed on the payroll several years.

It was an enjoyable recruitment because the people were so nice, the entire family, but it seemed as if it was taking every day of my life. Fortunately I was able to work two projects at once because Keith McCord was a sophomore at West End when T.R. was a senior and we ended up signing him in 1976.

Finally, it got down to the day I was supposed to sign T.R. I drove to Birmingham and when I arrived at their house, I saw Coach Smith and some other folks from North Carolina there. I took a gulp, rode around the block and sat and waited for them to leave.

At last, my turn came and I was relieved to learn they were waiting for me so he could sign an Alabama grant in aid. We got everybody seated and, lo and behold, I didn't have a pen with me. After two years of trying to get T.R. Dunn, I had to go next door and borrow a pen from one of their neighbors to get his signature on the line.

Two years before we signed T.R. Dunn, my main goal was to successfully recruit Charles Cleveland, a super athlete who played basketball, football and baseball at Brent High School near Centreville, Alabama. He was right down the road from Tuscaloosa, about thirty minutes, and I knew every bump along Highway 82.

Charles was an impact player from the word go, a 6-foot-5 guard, although he was unable to play with the varsity as a freshman because of the NCAA eligibility rule that was in place at that time. If he had been on that 1972 team that posted an 18-8 record without him, look out, it might have been NCAA Tournament bound.

Charles grew up the hard way. His family had little in the way of possessions. They struggled a lot and I felt for them. He was their pride and joy, rightfully so, and I know they smiled as broadly as I did when he got his degree from Alabama.

There was a little restaurant in Centreville called Twix and Tween, a super place to eat barbecue and sort of a local gathering place. We wanted to have a signing party for Charles there, do it in style, but the owner wouldn't let us. I'll let you guess why he wouldn't go for it.

But Charles got his turn in the spotlight shortly thereafter because we had massive crowds for freshman games. Everybody wanted to see him jump about two feet in the air while launching a 40-foot shot.

This next recruiting story is going to be extremely hard for me to relate because last weekend I attended Robert "Rah Rah" Scott's funeral. He died from stomach cancer while serving as an Alabama assistant coach on Coach Mark Gottfried's staff. I choose to remember "Rah Rah" as an energetic guard for Alabama from 1977 through 1980, twice a team captain and always a totally dedicated basketball player.

"Rah Rah" played at Parker High School in Birmingham under Coach Cap Brown, a great one. I drove to Birmingham day after day trying to get "Rah Rah" to commit to Alabama. It was a hard recruitment because I believe he enjoyed me chasing him so much and really had fun with it.

In fact, "Rah Rah" told the same story over and over, that I worried him so much he gave in. He told me one time the decisive blow was a day he was pitching in a high school baseball game. He said he was on the mound and looked at his catcher to get the sign for the next pitch. He said every time he saw the catcher crouched behind the plate he could see me behind the fence appearing as if I was looking over his shoulder. He said that's the day he threw in the towel, declared enough was enough and decided he would tell me he was going to sign with Alabama.

"Rah Rah" was a terrific young man and a terrific player. As a 6-foot-1 guard, he played on four teams that produced a combined 82-39 record. He became a basketball coach, winning a state championship at West End High School, and died as a basketball coach. The fact "Rah Rah" showed up for work while suffering with stomach cancer should tell you about his dedication and spirit. I'm sure he found comfort in a nice man like John Bostick visiting him frequently during his final weeks.

The UAB versus Alabama controversy reared its head again in a major way during the recruitment of Buck Johnson in 1983. That was one year after the Bobby Lee Hurt fiasco and the attacks on our program became more unreasonable.

I understood UAB was trying to get its program to a more recognizable position on the national level by improving its consistency. But I didn't understand then and I don't understand now why people associated with that program saw the need to be critical of everything we were doing in Tuscaloosa. Goodness, we had been around the block and had solidified our program to where it was getting wonderful national exposure.

Still, a smattering of people kept saying we should play UAB and more people wondered why we chose not to do that.

Well, here's the answer to that question.

I didn't see any reason to play UAB because if we had won it was something we were supposed to do and if we had lost it would've brought us closer together in recruiting. My principal thought was we should try to keep dominating the state when it came to signing prospects.

It wasn't that I didn't think UAB deserved a position within the state of Alabama, even the right to have a basketball program and attempt to let it grow. That was their business, pure and simple. But it was my business to do what was right for the University of Alabama and not to let UAB establish some type foothold in the state at our expense.

I didn't have a problem with UAB and I didn't have a problem with the UAB athletics director and basketball coach, although Gene Bartow seemed to have a lot of problems with me. I had no hard feelings toward him. If he had some toward me, well, that was his business.

My problem, the only one, was trying to take care of the Alabama basketball program so it could grow in stature. A way to do that was to intermingle teams like Georgetown, Michigan State, Duke, Maryland and others like that on our schedule with others we should have been able to defeat.

That plan worked for us in Tuscaloosa, as our success proves. We stayed on the course we designed, as political factions from Alabama and UAB battled on numerous issues. Basketball fans didn't understand all of the elements in the feud with UAB. A bunch of them just wanted us to play each other.

Now, after all these years, more than a decade and a half, I look back and think I was exactly right with the position I took.

The fact of the matter is UAB has started a football program, which it had every right to do, and they are competing with Alabama and Auburn for players while recruiting.

That stings football people in this state, those from Alabama and Auburn, because there's such a passion for that sport and always has been. Well, I had a passion for my sport, basketball, and I wasn't going to let that happen to the Crimson Tide program we had worked so hard to establish.

Anyway, back to the recruitment of Buck Johnson, it was an unusual situation. He was a fine player, a 6-foot-7 forward, and I really don't think he wanted to come to Alabama. Also, I don't think he wanted to play for me. I might be wrong, but I had that feeling. Still, it was my job to get the best talent we could if there was a remote chance it would work out right.

In some ways it did work out. Buck had some fine moments for us, leading us in scoring from 1984 through 1986 and in rebounds in 1984 and 1985. He played well for the Houston Rockets of the NBA. However, it was a struggle for both of us. I spent a lot of time during timeouts and practices trying to get him to listen to me and to play as hard as he was capable. There were times when he didn't seem to hear a word I was saying.

I think the reason for that is he wanted to go to UAB. But his mother thought Alabama was the best place for her son and she guided it. A lot of times parents won't do that because they don't want their son to be mad at them if it doesn't work out right. She wasn't afraid to state her opinion in his best interest.

Buck also had a grandmother who was a part of the process. She sat quietly through visits, but she didn't miss a thing and she probably had a lot to say after recruiters had gone home.

We reached a point where I thought it was a hopeless situation trying to get Buck to sign with us. I had pretty much resigned myself to UAB winning a recruiting battle against me. But one afternoon I was at home on the couch watching television and the telephone rang. Leroy McClendon said, "Coach, you won't believe this but I just signed Buck Johnson. The catch is he doesn't want to announce it right now. He wants to keep it a secret. He wants to visit some other schools."

I was ecstatic about us signing Buck because of all the time we had spent on him. But I didn't know how to handle the delay in an announcement. I knew we couldn't announce his signing, that he had to do that, and I didn't know what to think about him visiting other schools at their expense and wasting their coaches' time.

The next day I went in to see Coach Sam Bailey, who told me we could hold the scholarship without announcing it for three weeks. I tried to hide from the news media because I didn't want to lie to anybody. Finally, the story broke and an interesting recruitment came to a publicized end.

I absolutely loved recruiting Reginald King, a big strong guy from Jackson-Olin High School in Birmingham. The reason is he has always been a nice person and his mother, Mrs. Biddings, was a delight to be around. She came to a bunch of our home games, as a lot of mothers did, and she knew what the sport was about. She watched her son become the most prolific scorer in the history of Crimson Tide basketball.

I worked my fanny off recruiting Reggie. He was a determined 6-foot-6 forward who started as a freshman and kept on ticking. He had a good run as a professional player with the Kansas City Kings. He has been honored as a basketball legend in the Southeastern Conference.

Reggie had a most interesting shot, even when he was in high school. The basketball sort of floated toward the basket, looking like a knuckleball from baseball, and it went in many more times than not.

I'll never forget the first day Reggie participated in an Alabama basketball practice. The players went up and down the court a few times and C.M. Newton and I looked at each other and shook our heads, with our eyes wide. Neither of us had to say a word. We knew we had an outstanding talent to coach.

We spent a ton of time trying to get Reggie to come to Alabama. As he had been with T.R. Dunn, Frank Nix played a strong role. I believe he hired Reggie to work at his place during summer.

We were out front all the way with Reggie, who liked our style of play and knew a lot of our players, and we had an excited group when we went to sign him. We took a full crew to Birmingham for the occasion, including C.M. and his wife Evelyn and my wife Annette and me, because everybody loved Reggie and his mother.

Well, guess what we saw when we arrived at Reggie's house?

We saw a representative from another school standing on the front porch with something interesting in a hand. Immediately, I felt something funny was going on, that some offers were being made that weren't above board.

Thank goodness, Reggie and his mother didn't waver and he signed with us. He helped Alabama win 87 games. He scored 2,168 points and is the only Crimson Tide player to score 2,000 or more. He was SEC Player of the Year in 1978 and 1979. He had 1,279 rebounds, second with Leon Douglas to Jerry Harper in the history of the program.

The recruitment of Reggie King was tough, with it finally coming down to Alabama and Indiana.

But it was worth the effort, for sure, or as Reggie was fond of saying, for real.

CHAPTER TEN

Coaches and Characters in the SEC

*A strong Kentucky connection: Adolph Rupp, Joe B.
Hall and C.M. Newton in Tuscaloosa, Alabama*

There are numerous people who consider me one of the more weird characters who has coached basketball in the Southeastern Conference. That might be true, but it doesn't mean I've got a patent on eccentric behavior.

You'll probably come to the same conclusion after reading this chapter dedicated to faces seen and voices heard during my more than three decades at the University of Alabama. I won't come close to covering everybody because there have been what seems like a thousand coaches in the conference since 1960.

As I talk about some familiar and unfamiliar names, most of them coaches, and address the programs that make up the league, I'm sure you'll conclude I liked some and disliked some. That'll become more apparent when I get back to the 1980s in the next chapter, those glorious years I had with the Crimson Tide.

I don't know a better place for a guy who led Alabama to start a tour of the SEC than with Auburn, the tough intrastate rival.

Yes, there was a time I had what you could call a genuine distaste for Auburn. Hatred is too harsh a description, but not by much. My thinking has softened a lot since then. The change started when my dear friend Sonny Smith coached the Tigers and it picked up steam when Jimmy Rane of Great Southern Wood, a member of the Auburn Board of Trustees, hired me after I was ousted by Alabama.

Before I talk more about my feelings, let me set straight the record on why I once had hard feelings for Auburn and got so fired up for games against them.

There's no doubt Auburn had fine basketball under Coach Joel Eaves from 1950 through 1963. They had "Snow White and the Seven Dwarfs" and they ran an offense known as the "Auburn

Shuffle" that was difficult to defend and was highly successful. He had a 124-75 record. I've already told you how frustrating it was trying to beat them during the 1960s. In fact, they swept us, 6-0, from 1961 through 1963 and they recruited a lot of guys from our state and whipped us soundly in long stretches in the middle part of that decade.

One of the problems we had was the game was played in Montgomery, at Garrett Coliseum, and I've always considered that an Auburn city. They had a tremendous homecourt advantage down there. I begged our people to change it to a home and home arrangement, but Coach Hayden Riley and others didn't want to do that because it was such a bitter rivalry.

Finally, in 1968, Coach Riley's last season, we played them in Tuscaloosa, where we won, and in Auburn, where they won.

I didn't like us being dominated by the Tigers because it's important to beat an intrastate rival because of recruiting. But there are two more reasons I got so upset with Auburn.

From 1962 through 1964 we had a 6-foot-2 guard from Eufaula, Alabama named James Booth. Auburn had a player at least one of those years named Joe Newton, whose brother Bill Newton blocked two punts for the Auburn football team in 1972 to lead them to a 17-16 victory over Alabama.

In a game in Montgomery, I felt like Joe Newton intentionally ran under James Booth as he was attempting to shoot a layup and dumped him on the floor. It tore up his shoulder so bad he had to have surgery to get a pin placed in it. Joe Newton never came to our bench to check on James Booth. He never said he was sorry. That has been in my craw since that night and is the main reason I didn't like Auburn one iota most of the time I was coaching at Alabama.

Another reason is some things Bill Lynn said about Alabama. He was Auburn's coach from 1964 through 1973. He had a 7-3 record against Coach Riley, which isn't exactly what I'd call domination. Still, when C.M. Newton became our head coach in 1969, he had the gall to say he was going to kick Coach Newton in the butt just like he kicked Coach Riley in the butt.

That was too arrogant for my taste. It seemed a bit confrontational. Also, it needs to be stated Bill Lynn had a 6-4 record against us when C.M. was Alabama's coach and he lost his last four in 1972 and 1973, when we were on the comeback trail. In summary, Bill and Hayden Riley, good coaches, contributed mightily to the Alabama-Auburn rivalry.

That brings to mind a humorous story C.M. and I continue to laugh about, although it wasn't funny to me at the time.

As you know, it has been documented that I worked hard recruiting against Auburn, scouting Auburn and preparing Alabama teams for Auburn. In fact, I had "Beat Auburn" on my desk as a reminder of the importance, as if I needed one, and I got pretty emotional for about a week before we played the Tigers and during games against the Tigers.

Well, when C.M. arrived as coach, he made a change in the batting order, so to speak, and put Jock Sutherland in charge of the game plan for Auburn. It was his thinking that I got uptight and caused our players to get uptight. He didn't even let me go to the games. Instead, he put me on the road scouting the next opponent. This went on for a couple of years and, frankly, it didn't work. Finally, he put me back on the Auburn beat and allowed me to do some innovative things while attempting to motivate our players. The results in the series began turning our way.

C.M. told me a funny story once about Leon Douglas, our great center from 1973 through 1976, when we had a 7-1 record against Auburn. He said Leon stopped by his office one day and said, "Coach Newton, why do we hate Auburn so much?" C.M. explained to Leon why I got so fired up and bordered on going over the edge while getting our players ready for the Tigers.

Bob Davis coached Auburn from 1974 through 1978. He was

an interesting character who never made that much of an impact at a time when that program was trying to catch up with our program. He never beat us and was replaced by Paul Lambert, who died tragically after only two months in the position.

Then came a break for Auburn and a refreshing breeze for me, the arrival of Sonny Smith as coach. This was in the spring of 1978, about two years before I would become head coach at Alabama.

I'll tell you up front Sonny Smith and Hugh Durham, the former Georgia coach, are two of my better friends in the profession. We competed like crazy, along the lines of cats and dogs, but we laughed a lot, too. Sonny and I are still cackling, as anybody who listens to the sports radio talk show we host knows.

Sonny and I have known each other a long time, since our days as assistant coaches, me at Alabama and him at Virginia Tech, when we recruited against each other while trying to land top prospects. We were sort of an odd couple as head coaches at Auburn and Alabama. He's a delightfully funny guy, without trying to be, a native hillbilly type from Roan Mountain, Tennessee. His quick wit made him a favorite among sports writers. Meanwhile, I was considered an uptight grimacing type coach with the weight of the world on me. The fact is I could deliver funny lines, too, but only a few members of the news media took the time to notice.

It was like, hey, here's a smiling grown man named Sonny. He must be okay. And, oh no, here's a frowning grown man named Wimp. Something must have gone wrong in his life.

The truth is Sonny was as uptight as me, at least behind closed doors, and he agonized over losses just like I did.

When we do appearances together now that we're in rocking chairs and not uptight at all, Sonny likes to tell a story about me beating him so much while he was at Auburn. He talks about him getting three wishes that were guaranteed. He said he wanted a million dollars. The wish was granted but he was told ol' Wimp would get two million. He said he wanted a Mercedes automobile. The wish was granted but he was told ol' Wimp would get a Rolls Royce. With one more wish in hand, Sonny said, I want you to beat me half dead.

Auburn lost 11 straight games to Alabama between the 1976 season and the last part of the 1981 season. I was the head coach when Sonny ended that losing streak with a 56-54 victory over us down there. He won his share in head to head battles with me and got his program extremely competitive. We had a lot of give and take on the court during those years.

A little earlier I mentioned Sonny's Auburn team beat us in the finals of the SEC Tournament in 1985. That was after he had resigned as their coach, only to come back as their coach after that victory. He likes to tell people ol' Wimp kept alive his coaching career, let him live to go into another game. I don't remember putting that on my resume because the truth is Sonny was an excellent coach. He took Auburn to five consecutive NCAA Tournaments. That program has only been to seven NCAA Tournaments in its history.

But the Sonny and Wimp Show goes back much further than that, all the way to our assistant coaching days when we recruited against each other.

One of our favorite stories is about the recruitment of Charles "Boonie" Russell, a 6-foot-6 star forward at Alabama Christian College in Montgomery. It was a junior college then, 1974, and is a four-year college now. In fact, that's where my son Jim coaches.

Sonny was working for Virginia Tech, which a year earlier had won the National Invitation Tournament and had defeated Alabama, 74-73, in the semifinals. "Boonie" was going to visit Virginia Tech and then visit Alabama. He had pretty much made up his mind that one of us was going to be his choice.

When "Boonie" came to Tuscaloosa, I took the NIT program from the year previous and cut out every reference to Virginia

Tech. I put the program in a seat so he would start thumbing through it. I knew Sonny had told him Virginia Tech won the tournament and beat us en route to the finals, so I said, "'Boonie', I don't think that's right. I don't think Virginia Tech was in the NIT. There's the program, take a look for yourself."

Well, it wasn't long before I went to Montgomery and got "Boonie" to sign an Alabama grant in aid. But I didn't announce it to anybody.

Sonny tells the story best, but he was in Montgomery, too, and he had "Boonie" in a motel room still making a sales pitch on behalf of Virginia Tech. He had some food delivered for them. Then he turned on the television and saw the news report: "Alabama has signed Alabama Christian star Charles 'Boonie' Russell."

I don't know what Sonny was thinking at the time. But he still likes to tell that story and thinks it's funny.

We both lost one prospect, a super player up in Kentucky. As is the case with a lot of high school players, his parents didn't think he played enough and they were always complaining about it to Sonny and me. So we tried to use that while recruiting him, with me particularly interested in getting him out of that state because we had to compete with the Wildcats in the SEC. If he wasn't coming to Alabama, I wanted him at Virginia Tech.

We literally pooled our limited mental resources in an effort to come up with lines that would add fuel to the controversy over his playing time. We were sympathetic assistant coaches, or we made it appear that way, and one day I got so tickled about the lines we were coming up with I had to leave the high school gymnasium.

Kentucky signed him.

The recruitment of Robert Horry, a 6-foot-9 forward for us from 1989 through 1992, brought Sonny and I together face to face at a dominos table.

Every year, Andalusia, a little town in South Alabama, the Covington County seat, hosted the World Dominos Championship at Lurleen Wallace Junior College. I had gone down there a few times, basically because Coach Paul "Bear" Bryant went most years until his death and I was sort of a substitute from the University of Alabama. I always enjoyed the event because of its uniqueness and the charm those folks had, but I was particularly happy to be there when Robert Horry was starring at Andalusia High School.

Sonny was invited, too, and he wasn't going to miss the event because he was recruiting Robert as hard as I was. So we met down there with the tobacco chewers and snuff dippers in a big gymnasium. The prospect was there to watch us match wits at the dominos table.

As it worked out, Sonny got Miss Domino on his team, replete with a crown on her head, and I got some lady who was a friend of the college. They were supposed to help us through the game because, frankly, neither of us knew much about how to play.

I started mixing the bone yard, or shuffling the dominos for drawing, and I noticed Sonny was zeroing in on the double six. I wasn't even sure why that was important, but I noticed his eyes kept following that domino as I mixed them on the table. Meanwhile, I was keeping an eye on Robert Horry.

We played and I won. But Sonny told everybody he won and wanted me to tell a local newspaper reporter we tied. So when the guy came up to us to do an interview, we told him all three sides of the story. I'm not sure the reporter knew what to think when he left us.

I got Robert. Earlier, Sonny had beat me recruiting Charles Barkley.

I didn't expect to sign Charles Barkley, not after getting Bobby Lee Hurt and Ennis Whatley, but I wanted to make a strong bid. So I spent as much time as Sonny did in Leeds, Alabama recruiting a 6-foot-5 forward who would become one of the great players in NBA history. Also, UAB was still in the picture.

On our last visit, Leroy McClendon and I went to Charles' house and visited with his mother and him. Also, his grandmother was there, seated on a couch in a little sitting area adjacent to the living room. She was staying extremely quiet.

I pointed out I had gone to college in my hometown, at Florence State Teachers College, and because of that I didn't have much of a campus life. That was my way of getting UAB out of the way.

Then I pointed out the distance between Tuscaloosa and Leeds and Auburn and Leeds. I told Charles it was a lot closer to Tuscaloosa from Leeds than to Auburn from Leeds. I told Charles his mother and grandmother could attend a game in Tuscaloosa and be home safely by 11 p.m., but it would take them until 2 p.m. to get home from Auburn. That was my biggest sales pitch, that difference in travel time.

All of a sudden Charles' normally quiet grandmother said, "Coach Sanderson, Leeds is just as close to Auburn as it is Tuscaloosa if you drive over the mountain."

I looked at Leroy, put my little erroneous information in my brief case, shook hands with Charles and got ready to leave. I knew Sonny had beat me by telling them it was just as close to Auburn going over the mountain.

Now you see how my good buddy rarely missed a trick when it came to recruiting — the "Boonie" Russell episode being an exception.

I really think Sonny and I brought a little dignity to the Alabama-Auburn rivalry because of our friendship. The week of the game is an example of that because neither of us spent time talking down the other program. We didn't make accusations, at least not many, and that was different than in the past.

In summary, Sonny and I swapped licks, really got after each other while competing, shook hands and walked away from it. I'm thankful for that because he is a wonderful friend.

Earlier, I mentioned Hugh Durham, the former Georgia coach, is a dear friend, too. He's coaching at Jacksonville University now and I really miss seeing him prowling sidelines in the SEC.

Hugh and I go way back, too, to the years when he was an assistant coach and head coach at Florida State and I was an assistant coach at Alabama. I'm crazy about the guy because he's different than most coaches. He's an intelligent man, a native of Louisville, Kentucky, and he talks with a squeaky little voice that sounds more like a child than a man. He has a quick wit, too, and a good twinkle in his eyes. He has an ability to get in a good dig, even a serious statement about something bothering him, with a funny charm that softens the blow.

Interestingly, Hugh offered me an assistant coaching position at FSU after he became head coach. I went down and almost took the job. I backed out at the last minute and decided to stay at Alabama.

I think Hugh and I have always had a mutual respect. I know he's an excellent coach because he took Georgia to a Final Four in 1983, the year they beat us in the SEC Tournament championship game, and he had a 297-215 record at that school from 1979 through 1995. That isn't an easy place to be successful in basketball, not with the passion for football so strong.

Georgia doesn't have what could be termed a fabulous basketball tradition. The coaches just before Hugh in reverse order were John Guthrie, Ken Rosemond and Harbin Lawson. Those three guys worked hard in a tough environment, a state where football was more of a way of life.

I guess one of the things I remember most about playing games in Athens, Georgia for much of my time at Alabama was the old livestock arena or cow barn the Bulldogs called home. It wasn't an easy place to win because it was a long shot from being state of the art. In fact, when visiting teams were asked what end of the court they wanted in the first half most of them would take the wind.

Hugh Durham has a wonderful quick wit, like Sonny, and he was always on me about being so pessimistic and tightly wound. I remember a golf game we had once when I hit an eight-iron shot in the hole on my second shot for an eagle. Hugh quickly said all I was thinking about when the ball went in was I wouldn't hit another shot that good the rest of round.

One of the funnier things that happened involving Hugh and me came while both of us were recruiting Allen Murphy, a great forward from Birmingham and one of the better high school players in the nation. Hugh was at Florida State, as head coach, and it seemed to get down to Alabama, FSU and Auburn. There were no limits on visits then and we were all in there buying meals for him and his family and, more or less, involved in a merry chase that got bizarre.

Meanwhile, Louisville had just hired Denny Crum as its coach and he joined the pursuit of Allen Murphy.

We considered hiring Herman Williams, a great high school coach and Allen's coach, in an effort to land both of them in Tuscaloosa.

Herman went to Dilliard College in Louisiana to make a speech and he took Allen with him. All of the coaches recruiting Allen were at a barbecue place in Birmingham waiting for them to return. I was in Tuscaloosa because I had convinced Herman to bring Allen to campus en route from Louisiana to Birmingham.

I tried everything to get Allen to sign with Alabama. He wouldn't do it. But he told me he was going to make a decision that night and asked me to follow him back to Birmingham.

I hurried in and told C.M. we needed to go to Birmingham, that Allen Murphy was about make a move. He wasn't excited about it because it wasn't his nature to hang around a guy and beg him. But he consented and we went to Birmingham and checked into a room at the Red Carpet Inn.

I had worked on Allen Murphy for two years, mighty hard, and had spent hours with him. In fact, we ate at the same restaurant so many times he didn't need a menu to order. He just said, "Bring me Number 3, medium well." It was a circus and it seemed like it was about to end. I wanted to sign him and get home.

After C.M. and I got settled, I decided to go see Allen that evening. It was sprinkling rain and was kind of chilly. When I got there I saw four or five Florida State players, Florida State cheerleaders and Florida State coaches in the living room. The place was packed and it seemed the only person who wasn't there was Allen. So I hung around, standing in the rain, and waited for him to arrive. Then I slipped in the back door of his house.

There we were, Hugh Durham and Wimp Sanderson, face to face with each other with a highly touted prospect we both wanted. Hugh had me outnumbered badly, with the cheerleaders and players there, but I was trying to protect our interest.

I said, "Allen, have you signed with anybody?"

He said, "No sir, Coach Sanderson, not with anybody."

I left Hugh and his crowd with Allen and returned to the motel. The next morning I drove to the house, knocked on the door, said hello and stepped inside.

At that moment, Allen's mother said, "Coach Sanderson, Allen has signed with Louisville. We're going to get some pictures made and we'd like for you to stay and be in them."

I said, "No thank you, ma'am. I believe I'll pass on that opportunity."

I've wondered what the portrait she really wanted would have looked like with Coach Crum smiling, me scowling and Hugh Durham and those players and cheerleaders he had with him all around us.

You can be sure the Allen Murphy episode almost killed me — literally.

Auburn had driven Allen and his mother to campus for a visit and I was sitting in my car about a block away waiting for them to get back. When they showed up I got out of my car and crawled through some bushes on my belly to see what was going on.

I saw some interesting things, too, and was waiting for the Auburn coach to leave. The wind was howling and it blew open the door to their house at about the time a Brown Service Funeral Home vehicle was approaching.

They all came outside, I think to pay a burial insurance policy premium, and when they did I made my move. Ultimately, I ended up inside the Murphy's house.

There I was, growing more weary by the moment, but still willing to protect our interest in Allen Murphy.

It's safe to say Dale Brown, the former LSU coach, is one of the unique individuals in the history of college basketball. He was never bashful about stating an opinion. He remains an interesting person who had a lot of success in Baton Rouge.

Dale was always on a campaign of some type, at times a renegade, and he was a walking and talking philosopher who thought motivation was the ultimate tool in coaching. For several years not a month went by without him sending me sheets of paper with inspirational phrases, stories or poems on them. I saw a lot of LSU purple ink during that time.

When Dale arrived at LSU in 1973, the program had fallen on hard times. Interest was at ground zero. So he traveled around the state in a car and put purple and yellow nets on every basketball goal he found. That's the type energy and promotional savvy he had. A lot of people rolled their eyes and thought he was a nut, but none of us were laughing when he took the Bengal Tigers to 13 NCAA Tournaments between 1979 and 1993. That run included the Final Four in 1981 and 1986.

Dale has always said he was an underdog fighting to overcome long odds to become a successful coach. He did overcome a tough upbringing and a down period at LSU and, by all means, the word character fits him perfectly.

Dale could make people mad. In fact, he has the distinction of making C.M. Newton as mad as I've ever seen him.

LSU had never won an outright SEC championship until 1979, having shared a couple with Kentucky, the most recent in 1954. So there was a lot of excitement in Baton Rouge when we went down there to play in the latter stages of that season.

We were struggling and they were on a roll. They beat us, 86-66, really waxed us. But that's just a small part of the story.

Late in the game, as we were just trying to get it over with and get to the dressing room to lick our wounds, Dale called a timeout. Instead of talking to his team, he stood in front of the bench and motioned for some character in the rafters overhead to unfurl a banner that said something like "LSU: SEC Champions!" Their fans went crazy and held up the conclusion of the game.

C.M. was extremely upset, as mad as I had ever seen him. I'll never forget the following morning at the hotel in which we were staying. We were about to get on a bus for a ride to Oxford, Mississippi for our next game when Dale showed up in the lobby. He attempted to apologize to C.M. and he didn't get far in that regard. They discussed the evening before and I'm not sure much was settled.

I've always gotten along fine with Dale. I've recognized his peculiarities and figured I've got some, too. However, I got in his doghouse in 1990 and I'm not sure I'm out of it for keeps.

That was one of the seasons he had Shaquille O'Neal on his team and during the SEC Media Day during preseason practice I made an effort to be funny. I said, "Dale's team is so good even he can't screw it up." Well, sports writers laughed and laughed. Unfortunately, Dale didn't think it was funny.

Dale wrote me a letter voicing his displeasure with that statement. I wrote him a letter and told him I didn't mean anything uncomplimentary. I telephoned him and apologized. I begged him for forgiveness. Every time I'd see him he'd say something about that statement. I kept begging him to forgive me.

Even after "Shaq" was gone, the same year I was about to be asked to leave, Dale kept saying, "Wimp, you know I beat you five straight games after you made that statement."

My favorite Dale Brown memory comes from the 1987 SEC Tournament when we beat LSU, 69-62, at The Omni in Atlanta, Georgia.

In keeping with his norm, Dale was on a mission at that event. He had a pretty good team, 24-15, but it had struggled through the early part of the SEC regular season and had a low seed in the tournament. So since LSU had to win four games in four days to win the championship, he vowed fatigue wouldn't be a factor and promised not to sleep until the tournament was over.

Dale was attempting to motivate his players, as he said teaching them the power of positive thinking in the wake of utter exhaustion. That ploy made national headlines and everybody was talking about it in Atlanta. I really didn't know what the fuss was over because I was interested only in getting our outstanding team, 28-5, through the tournament.

After beating Tennessee in the first round, Auburn in the semifinals and LSU in the finals, I was a happy camper when I got to the news media interview room after we had cut down the nets. That's when I told sports writers, "I went by the LSU bench to shake hands with Dale before the game but he was sound asleep."

I think Dale even laughed that day.

In summary, there's no way to tell what's going on in Dale Brown's mind. He continues to call me to talk about worldwide issues or trends in sports. He's really a good guy, I think, just a whole lot different.

Earlier in this book I told you a story about Adolph Rupp, the great coach at Kentucky and the man everybody thinks about first when SEC basketball is mentioned. He coached 41 years, from 1931 through 1972. His record was 876-190, a winning percentage of 82.2.

Only Dean Smith of North Carolina has won more games than the "Baron of the Bluegrass" — his record was 879-254, 77.6 percent — and only Clair Bee has a better winning percentage, 82.6 with a 412-87 record.

Coach Rupp won 27 SEC championships, four NCAA Tournament championships and one National Invitation Tournament championship. That should tell you for a long time the conference was Kentucky and the rest of us.

I've got a lot of vivid memories of going to Lexington, Kentucky to play games, some good and most of them bad, because going against the Wildcats in old Memorial Gym and spacious Rupp Arena was a challenge and an experience. That wasn't just when Coach Rupp was there, either, because Joe Hall, who followed him, kept that program rolling, as did Eddie Sutton, Rick Pitino and Tubby Smith.

An exceptional trivia question would be can you name one of the three coaches at Kentucky prior to Adolph Rupp. The answer is John Mauer, Bash Hayden or Ray Eklund. Of course, you know that, huh?

Well, a lot of Kentucky fans might have scored on that question because it's amazing how intelligent they are when it comes to basketball and how supportive they are of the Big Blue. At games up there you hear the crowd roar a split second before an official blows his whistle to signal a walking violation or a personal foul. I think most coaches appreciate that type interest among fans and I think most of our players liked going into that type environment.

Kentucky, North Carolina, Kansas, Indiana and UCLA are the most traditional names in college basketball and I'm honored to have coached against all of them except Kansas. I'm thankful, too, because I survived a long time going against the Wildcats when most coaches aren't so fortunate.

Coaches in the SEC will tell you there isn't anything more challenging that playing against Kentucky every year. It's a thoroughbred program from top to bottom. I lost four times to them in 1986, twice during the regular season, once in the SEC Tournament and once in the NCAA Tournament. However, Alabama had its share of success, too, which makes games against the Wildcats memorable. I think they respected us.

At first blush, those 22 wins and 44 losses don't look impressive. But Kentucky lost only 248 games during those 32 years, an average of fewer than eight times per season, so we tagged them with our share.

Coach Rupp started the dominance and it has lingered for quite a while.

Interestingly, C.M. is the only one of Coach Rupp's former players to defeat him as a coach. That happened in 1972, when Alabama won, 73-70, in Tuscaloosa after they beat us, 77-74, in Lexington. Coach Rupp was upset about that loss, really did get mad, and, ironically, it came during his last season.

Not long before he died, Coach Rupp came to Tuscaloosa to address the Alabama High School Athletic Association Coaches Convention we were hosting on campus. That took a lot of effort because he got out of bed to make the trip and flew on an airplane equipped with a specially designed stretcher. He thought that much of C.M. Newton.

I don't know many stories related to Coach Rupp that I can tell you. But I've heard some wonderful ones from C.M., one definitely worth relating.

Kentucky's chief rival for a long time was Tennessee. One year "Wah Wah" Jones was playing for the Wildcats and his brother was playing for the Vols. In the dressing room before the game Coach Rupp said, "I want you to know everybody in Knoxville is a 100-karat son of a b——, except your brother, 'Wah-Wah'."

That's how it was with Coach Rupp, I'm told, a little coarse at times and demanding all of the time. It has been said officials became apprehensive at times when making calls in Lexington with him seated on the bench.

As I've said, there was time long ago when Alabama and Kentucky used to fight tooth and nail and had some great games, like in the 1930s, when it was common for from two to six points to be the margin of victory or defeat in Lexington. However, for some reason Coach Hank Crisp wasn't at courtside to lead the Crimson Tide during a game up there and the Wildcats blitzed their way to a massive halftime lead. I've been told that instead of spending the entire break with his team, Coach Rupp went to the Crimson Tide dressing room and drew up some plays for the opposition.

That's the only time I've heard of that happening, an opposing coach helping the other team. But there has always been a special mutual respect between Alabama and Kentucky.

I certainly respect that program. I think their fans respected the way our players performed.

Speaking of respect, I have a ton of it for Joe Hall and what he accomplished coaching Kentucky from 1973 through 1985. He got the job after serving under Coach Rupp for several years and it was a tough act to follow, something like Coach Ray Perkins faced following Coach Paul "Bear" Bryant as football coach at Alabama.

Joe was a strong disciplinarian and almost a perfectionist who didn't like to see players fail to reach potential. His fiery sidecourt antics are legendary. But he got results, posting a 297-

100 record and winning a national championship in 1978.

Joe was always under scrutiny. No matter what he did it didn't seem to be good enough for Kentucky fans. They were even critical after he left coaching and took a job at a bank in Lexington. Some supporters heard he had accepted that position and said, "Now it'll be easy to rob that bank because Joe won't let the guards shoot."

Eddie Sutton did a nice job coaching at Kentucky, too, but the Wildcats went to greater heights under Rick Pitino. His pressing defense was outstanding and he prepared teams extremely well. Frankly, I had a hard time beating him, winning twice in six games when he was in Lexington and I was in Tuscaloosa.

Rick was a different type person and wasn't particularly friendly with me. In fact, after I was forced out of my position during the spring of 1992, he's the only coach from the conference who didn't telephone me, which is fine, I guess.

But I must relate one interesting story about Rick that indicated he noticed what we were doing at Alabama.

When we went to Kentucky to play one year, I got a telephone call from a local tailor who asked if I'd be offended in any way if Rick wore a plaid sport coat during the game. Obviously, he intended to discard one of his expensive designer suits for one night because I usually wore plaid.

I didn't voice an objection, simply said that was fine with me, and he entertained fans showing up in plaid.

I didn't have the opportunity to coach against Tubby Smith after his arrival at Kentucky. But I've really been impressed with what he has done with that program in three seasons.

Two of the more unique characters in SEC basketball history were Ray Mears, the Tennessee head coach from 1963 through 1977, and his longtime assistant coach Stu Aberdeen. They were a competitive pair who earned our respect, only in a little different way than Kentucky did.

Ray Mears was an outstanding coach at Whittenberg College and arrived at Tennessee at a time when they were attempting to revamp the basketball program after 12-11, 10-15 and 4-19 records. It didn't take him long to accomplish the task. He had 13-11, 16-8, 20-5, 18-8 and 21-7 records his first five years, with the last one resulting in a SEC championship. He had a 278-112 record leading the Volunteers.

Tennessee under Mears was different, for sure. The offense was a 1-3-1 that would put people to sleep with its passing and dribbling and little shooting. The defense was a zone almost all the time, which also kept scoring to a minimum. But it was a spectacle more than anything, with him using all types of ploys while motivating his players and exciting the fans up there.

The players busted through a big paper 'T' when running onto the court before games. They were introduced under a bright spotlight. They had a player who rode a unicycle on the court during warmups. They had the Ernie and Bernie Show named after Ernie Grunfeld and Bernard King, two great players.

The sight of all that orange and all of that hoopla was shocking to most visiting teams. We saw it enough to get used to it.

Mears and Aberdeen were intense individuals. Before games in Knoxville they would stand in your way so you couldn't watch your team warm up. They were there to compete and they didn't mind if you knew it. They did a lot of it for show, a way to motivate the Vols. However, there were nights in Stokely Athletics Center when sportsmanship seemed to fly out of the window, especially if we beat Tennessee. Ray took losing harder than anybody I've encountered, including me.

Alabama and Tennessee have pretty much broken even through the years in wins and losses, with the Crimson Tide leading by a few. But Ray Mears really took it personal when we had strong runs against them. We won seven of 10 meetings from

1972 through 1976, five straight at one point, and his reaction was to practice his team all of one season wearing shirts with "Beat Bama" in crimson on them.

Ray is a good person, I believe, and an excellent coach who was good for the sport. However, he was quite different when you got him around a basketball court and a game against a rival was going on.

Ray had an aura about him. As an example, Sonny Smith told me he ran into him at a basketball clinic somewhere and he needed a ride back to his hotel. Sonny told him, sure, hop in and Ray got in the back seat like he expected to be chauffeured.

Ray beat us twice his last season, 1977, and given our 25-6 record that year I'm sure he has reflected on that happily during his time away from coaching.

As for me, after a slow start, 1-3 and 4-5, I'll take my 18-8 record against Tennessee and go to the house.

From 1979 though 1989, Tennessee had a prince of a coach in Don DeVoe. I hated to see him depart there because he was a pleasure to be around, even though he was a fierce competitor during games. He's at the U.S. Naval Academy now and doing well. That seems like an ideal place for a man like him because he insisted on discipline and drove his players like a drill sergeant.

Oh me, where do I start while reflecting on stormin' Norm Sloan, the former Florida coach who arrived there after a successful run at North Carolina State? Maybe I should just say he was stormy, all the time complaining about this or that.

Norm was a little difficult to get along with and didn't seem to be comfortable unless some kind of controversy was surrounding him. He stayed mad about something all of the time.

Norm took two turns at Florida, from 1961 through 1966, and 1982 through 1989. He got his last three teams to the NCAA Tournament, to his credit. He did an outstanding job for a long time. The folks down there would have to confirm it, but I'd guess the enthusiasm he created for basketball during those seasons was something new for the Gators' fans.

While on the subject of Florida, that has always been a tough place to visit when it comes to basketball. For what seems like forever, the home team played in Alligator Alley, a pint sized gymnasium with barely enough room to turn around. A lot of exceptional teams have gone in there and lost to inferior teams. We took our share of shots at Alabama during the 1970s, losing down there five times. Then when they built a new gym, the O'Connell Center, it was a big bubble with 12,000 seats and a roof that is supported by air. They even have an aquatics center in the building.

Things have changed substantially at Florida since the 1960s, 1970s and 1980s, when there was a revolving door in place reserved for coaches. Tommy Bartlett lasted from 1967 through 1973 and John Lotz lasted from 1974 through 1980, when an interesting character named Ed Visscher completed the last 14 games of the final season. Then came Norm Sloan and, surprisingly, Don DeVoe for 18 games of the 1980 season.

Players walked out in droves, too, a real mutiny, but as of this writing Coach Billy Donovan has stabilized that situation.

Mississippi State is another program that was slow developing its athletics department facilities and I've been a part of a bunch of games in an old gym they called The Barn or something like that. And, gracious, I can't complete a rundown of characters from the SEC without talking about Eugene "Babe" McCarthy.

McCarthy coached Mississippi State from 1956 through 1965. He had four conference championship teams, in 1959, 1961, 1962 and 1963. Two of those teams lost only one game and a lot of people consider him a master of some form.

I'll just say he was a confident individual who knew how to coach the slowdown offense extremely well.

I'm sure a lot of people are familiar with a game Mississippi State played against Kentucky in which the Bulldogs attempted eight shots in the first half and made seven. Then after winning the victors put a wreath around a goal on the court in Lexington, Kentucky.

I'm telling you "Babe" McCarthy could really get next to Coach Rupp, infuriating him in a variety of ways.

I had an interesting exchange with McCarthy once during my early years at Alabama and ended up having the last laugh.

I took the Alabama freshman team to Starkville one year for a truly hardfought game. They had a couple of guys from campus officiating and I didn't like the way they handled their duties. I got upset and said some things, really let them have it.

Maybe I shouldn't have said anything, but I was young and eager, as well as ferociously competitive.

After the game, "Babe" McCarthy had a few choice words for me. Among them was a vow that we wouldn't beat his teams.

Well, that made me work mighty hard helping Coach Hayden Riley prepare for games against Mississippi State. As I said earlier, we beat them a few times in Tuscaloosa and I'll never forget the night "Babe" McCarthy got upset after a loss to us and threw his watch across the court at Foster Auditorium.

Come to think of it, he might have thrown it to the floor and stomped on it.

Joe Dan Gold followed McCarthy at Mississippi State and stayed five seasons. Then came Kermit Davis, who lasted from 1971 through 1977.

Through the changes, the Bulldogs were never soft touches.

Incredulously, a lively character named Ron Greene arrived as Mississippi State's coach in 1979. He promptly posted an 18-9 record, 13-5 in the conference, and resigned. We whipped his team in Tuscaloosa, 87-65, then barely got away with a victory in Starkville, 68-67, in a wild one.

Jim Hatfield coached Mississippi State three seasons and Bob Boyd coached the Bulldogs five seasons.

I've got to say something about Bob Boyd, an interesting character who had coached Southern Cal to a string of second place finishes to Coach John Wooden and UCLA in the Pacific Ten Conference, which at that time was the Pac-Eight. That was a great disservice for a masterful teacher because if he had done that in this era he would have taken the Trojans to many NCAA Tournaments in a row because the field has grown so large.

Also, Coach Boyd and USC won a few times over Coach Wooden and UCLA, probably more than anybody else. That doesn't surprise me because he ran an offense that was difficult to defend and, for all practical purposes, he got Mississippi State turned in the right direction again.

Then came stability in Starkville with the arrival of my friend Richard Williams, who between 1987 and 1998 coached Mississippi State to three NCAA Tournament appearances and two National Invitation Tournament appearances. He won conference championships in 1991 and 1996, with the latter team advancing to the Final Four.

We split with the Bulldogs in 1991.

Richard did a magnificent job coaching Mississippi State from 1987 through 1998.

Now I'll tell you a decision I made several years ago that has led to a longlasting and warm friendship.

Not long after Mississippi State hired Richard as its coach, we were at the SEC Spring Meeting in Destin, Florida. I knew Richard was the type guy who stayed to himself, sort of shy, and for some reason I thought he might be nervous about the series of meetings that were to start the next day. So Annette and I asked Diann and Richard if they wanted to go to dinner with us.

Well, that was a great decision. I discovered a wonderful friend, to go with a great basketball coach, and Diann, Richard,

Annette and I attempted to have an enjoyable dinner together in Destin, Florida every year after that.

One of the fine quiet men in SEC basketball history is Roy Skinner, who coached Vanderbilt in 1959 and from 1962 through 1976. It was an honor being in Memorial Gymnasium the evening he coached his final game for the Commodores. It was a great game, too, as Alabama won in overtime, 84-77, and the fans in Nashville said farewell to a popular man.

Roy always had his teams ready to play, as his 278-135 record indicates. He led Vanderbilt to an outright conference championship in 1965 and they tied us for the crown in 1974. I won't forget that year for as long as I live because the Commodores beat us 73-72 in Nashville and 67-65 in Tuscaloosa, gut wrenching losses.

Roy Skinner was followed at Vanderbilt by Wayne Dobbs, a nice man, and for three seasons the Commodores' fans loved his colorful antics.

Richard Schmidt was the Vanderbilt coach for two seasons and was replaced despite winning one more game than he lost. He was a victim of circumstance, I guess, because he was there when the Commodores had the opportunity to hire my former boss, C.M. Newton, who was ready to leave the SEC Office.

C.M. and I went at it for eight years and I don't think either of us really enjoyed the competition.

We had some great games and I'd be untruthful if I said the ones we won weren't meaningful. I think that's a natural reaction and, although he can speak for himself, I think C.M. felt the same way. I know for a fact he was emotional when he brought his first team to Memorial Coliseum.

A lot of my friends remember one of our losses by a basket at Vanderbilt, in 1983 or 1984, because when the buzzer sounded I went face down in front of the bench, like I had been shot in the forehead with a pistol.

C.M. had some good teams at Vanderbilt, a couple I'd term exceptional. Of course, he was there from 1982 through 1989, when I was fortunate to have some super players and some outstanding teams.

In summary, I'll always think those games were marked by familiarity, not the type that breeds contempt, rather the type that produces respect.

The familiarity became a little perplexing at one point because there was a period during C.M.'s time at Vanderbilt when he had two of my former assistant coaches on the bench with him. It was natural for John Bostick to be there because he and C.M. had worked so long together at Alabama. But it was a little strange that Leroy McClendon was there.

I've told you what Leroy meant to our program at Alabama, particularly in the recruiting area. Well, one day he came to me and said C.M. had telephoned him to let him know Bob Weltlich was interested in him joining his staff at Texas. Leroy thought about it and, after a couple of days, came into my office and said, "Coach, I'm going to stay at Alabama."

At some point Leroy came back into my office and said C.M. thought he at least needed to talk to Bob Weltlich. Leroy did that and joined the Texas staff. Well, the next thing I knew Leroy was on C.M.'s staff at Vanderbilt working hard to beat us.

I'd be less than honest if I said that whole deal didn't bother me.

One of the characters I'll never forget is Bonnie "Country" Graham, who coached at Ole Miss from 1950 through 1962. He was country, no doubt, a real backwoods sounding guy, and in those years the Rebels played home games in a little gym upstairs in one of the buildings on campus. They were never particularly good, but they were hard to beat in that environment.

Coach Hayden Riley had me scouting during my first two years at Alabama and that makes me remember something that sort of points out the lack of emphasis folks put on SEC basketball during those years.

Our team was playing at Ole Miss and I arrived in Columbus, Mississippi to meet the coaches and players after going on a scouting trip. As I recall, we were going to play Mississippi State in nearby Starkville on Monday night after playing the Rebels on Saturday night.

I went to check in late at night and asked the desk clerk how the Alabama-Ole Miss basketball game had come out. He told me without hesitation that Ole Miss had won and that disgusted me. I went to bed that night tossing and fretting about us losing for the eighth time in a row, albeit to a team we should have beaten.

I still had a bad taste in my mouth the next morning when I went to get some coffee and, lo and behold, found out Alabama had defeated Ole Miss, 68-62, to end that losing streak.

I know it seems strange that I would include that desk clerk in memorable characters from my years coaching in the SEC. Heck, I don't even know his name. But that guy put me through a lot of misery that night when I should have had the time to enjoy the only road game the Crimson Tide won that season.

Believe me, going on the road in the SEC back then is a whole lot different than it is now.

Basically, in the 1960s you got on a bus and traveled back roads, interstate highways when they were available, and you stayed in cheap motels. In the 1970s, we started flying more, but in old Southern Airlines planes that were cramped and, truthfully, so breezy you could smell the fuel as it propelled the engines. Sometimes we traveled by chartered plane and sometimes we went the commercial route. The overnight accommodations got better because we had more money in the budget and could stay at the Campbell House in Lexington, Kentucky, the Hilton Hotel in Baton Rouge, Louisiana and Gainesville, Florida and the Hyatt Regency Hotel in Knoxville, Tennessee. It was the Holiday Inn most every other place.

But those were fun times, moving around the conference, and I'll never forget watching many of our players making their first flights and several news media members and basketball staff members playing loud games of gin rummy.

As for me, as an assistant coach I was too concerned about the games to be played to relax much. I'd spend time going over notes, the scouting report, and after we arrived on a given campus I did a lot of walking in an effort to relieve anxiety.

Little did I know then, during the 1960s and 1970s, that I would be in charge of the program when we played games in Hawaii, Japan and Puerto Rico.

CHAPTER ELEVEN

The 1980s: A Decade to Remember

(Continued)

A definite highlight of the Wimp Sanderson Era was the SEC Tournament championship in 1987, the year the Crimson Tide also won the regular season championship

On October 15, 1985 there was an air of confidence surrounding the University of Alabama basketball program that was enlightening.

Wimp Sanderson, the coach, felt much more at ease than during earlier years. We had reached a nice level of success and wanted to build on it. We had just participated in four consecutive NCAA Tournaments and had not embarrassed ourselves. What is more, we had some fine players at our disposal, not necessarily superstars, rather young men who blended together remarkably well as a team. Almost all of them were coachable, meaning they would listen to us during practice and carry out game plans.

We had sold our players on a good goal, making it to the Final Four, and to a man they thought that was a noble and possible achievement. I could tell that by the way they worked at practice, by the way they conducted themselves while out of the spotlight, and I wanted to make that come true for them.

Our fans were delightful. They were giving Alabama basketball the type support it deserved and, more importantly, it needed. At last, they knew the Crimson Tide feared nobody, not a national champion and not a traditional power.

I thought our recruiting effort was extremely good during that time, with thanks to some assistant coaches who worked extremely hard, and the influx of new players year in and year out added to what I perceived to be a strong foundation.

We were at a point, I think, where we could compete on a consistent basis, thus adding to our tradition and, of course, developing an even stronger sales pitch for prospects.

Our family was living in Woodland Hills and Annette and I really enjoyed watching the boys grow up.

It was a time of reflection, good soul searching, and it was a time for anticipation, good goals — higher than had ever been involved with the Alabama basketball program.

We were on top of things in 1986, with a 24-9 record overall and a 13-5 Southeastern Conference record. We had developed good depth. Buck Johnson was a senior. Derrick McKey was an out of this world junior. Jim Farmer and Terry Coner, both proven players, were junior guards. Mark Gottfried was a junior and ready to contribute. Craig Dudley, a good little guard, was a sophomore after rehabilitating a bad injury, a real worker who could play. Michael Ansley was a freshman forward and, as best I could tell at the time, ready to knock people around inside.

We won our first six games, dropped one at Maryland, 60-58, and headed to El Paso, Texas for the Sun Bowl Tournament. After getting past Nebraska, 78-61, we played Coach Don Haskins' Texas-El Paso team for the championship.

It was a wild affair, a rare occasion when things got totally out of hand on the court. I looked up at one point and Don Haskins was down in front of our bench coaching his team, about as far out of his box as he could get. Then a fight broke out and Buck Johnson got kicked out of the game.

They beat us, 74-62, and I don't know what good we got out of it unless it was learning to defend ourselves on an opposing floor. Maybe it toughened us up, but you couldn't tell it because we started conference play with a 2-2 record, looking impressive at Mississippi State and against LSU and looking terrible at Georgia and at Kentucky.

Then we went on an eight-game winning streak, not really challenged, before Kentucky beat us by two points at home and Auburn beat us by two points on the road.

The SEC Tournament was in Lexington, Kentucky that season, which wasn't comforting for a coach who had seen his team lose twice to the Wildcats. I found some relief knowing the only way we would meet them was in the finals and that's what happened after we beat Georgia, 79-59, and Mississippi State, 77-65, in the semifinals.

The victory over Mississippi State came in Bob Boyd's last game as coach. I really hated to see him leave the SEC because he was a breath of fresh air in a highly competitive league, a man who enjoyed a good laugh and made people smile with his extremely quick wit.

Kentucky got us for the third time in the finals, 83-72, although we played pretty good against a team that posted a 32-4 record. That was Coach Eddie Sutton's first year in Lexington and he had the natives excited.

That Kentucky team was led by Kenny Walker, who got good support from Winston Bennett and Roger Harden, a hardnosed guard.

The postseason was bizarre because after a couple of rounds in the NCAA Tournament conference sisters Alabama, Kentucky and LSU all ended up in Atlanta, Georgia.

We went to Charlotte, North Carolina for the first two games and beat Xavier, 97-80, and Illinois, 58-56.

We played excellent basketball and our young team was coming into its own. All of the players I mentioned earlier were doing well at that point and, as a bonus, little J.J. Jackson, a 5-foot-11 junior guard, started contributing a little more than he had.

Obviously, the game with Illinois, a fine team from the Big Ten Conference, came down to the wire and Terry Coner made a shot at the buzzer to win it. It was amazing how he did that so many times, got a bucket when we sorely needed one. An ability to score like that is often the difference in an excellent point guard and a great point guard. He had it all, could even rebound.

After the game, Lou Hensen, the Illinois coach, came by and asked me if I thought Terry had traveled before making the last shot. I told him it was close, that I didn't know if he did or not.

The euphoria we experienced in Charlotte didn't last long because we were face to face with Kentucky again in the Sweet Sixteen. I couldn't believe the tournament committee could draw up brackets as ridiculous as that. Not only was Kentucky there, but LSU was, too, and to top it off Georgia Tech was the other team playing within the shadows of its campus.

We lost to Kentucky, 68-63, close but no cigars. LSU beat Georgia Tech, 70-64. Then the Bengal Tigers beat Kentucky, 59-57, to advance to the Final Four.

I don't know if Alabama and Kentucky were good enough to make it to the Final Four, but I'll always wonder how far our 1986 team could have gone had the NCAA Tournament bracket made a little more sense. That thing really blew my mind. There were four SEC teams in the field that year, with Coach Sonny Smith advancing his Auburn team to the Elite Eight in Houston, Texas, and, son of a gun, three of us end up in the same building because we won two games to get there.

It was a strange postseason because the two teams with the poorer records, Auburn at 22-11, and LSU at 26-12, went further in the NCAA Tournament than the two teams who played in the SEC Tournament championship game and had the better records. Making matters more agonizing for me was the fact Kentucky beat us four times.

The SEC was changing its face a little as every program attempted to upgrade its basketball stature. For instance, the 1986 season produced a top six consisting of Kentucky, Alabama, Auburn, Florida, LSU and Georgia. The truth is there wasn't any easy place to play. Fortunately, we had the type players who were seasoned enough to be competitive in any setting.

I've never liked to compare basketball teams or players to determine if one is better than the other. In other words I'm not into selecting an all-Alabama team among the players I coached.

But I must say the 1987 Alabama team was one of the better

ones in the history of the program. Those guys produced a 28-5 record and two of the losses were by one point. They won 19 of 21 SEC games, counting the tournament championship, and they won on the road in a lot of hostile environments.

We put a heck of a starting lineup on the court, with Derrick McKey at center, Michael Ansley and Jim Farmer at the forwards and Terry Coner and Mark Gottfried at the guards. We could change it up, too, inserting Keith Askins at forward and letting Jim Farmer take a turn at guard. J.J. Jackson added depth at guard.

All of those inside players spent some time in the National Basketball Association. All of those guards were smart and rarely made miscues. In fact, Terry Coner might go down as one of the greater guards in the history of Alabama basketball. He played defense. He passed to the open man. He got rebounds. He made shots when he had to. He was a pleasure, a vital part of an outstanding group.

That team was a machine of sorts and it played well together. Also, it was a totally unselfish group. I think other coaches thought we had a fine team.

Interestingly, the 1987 Alabama team lost two of its first five games, by a point at Florida State and by nine points to Duke in East Rutherford, N.Y. But after that, look out, because there were 12 consecutive wins before Florida beat us in overtime down there. When Kentucky defeated us at home, 70-69, after we had won up there, 69-55, the outcome was considered an upset.

Our final regular season game that season was against Florida in Tuscaloosa. There have been a lot of thrilling games in Alabama basketball history, like a 93-90 victory over Tennessee in two overtimes in 1976 and a 101-100 loss to Kentucky in the 1979 SEC Tournament. But I'm not sure the 86-85 victory we had over the Gators in overtime in 1987 wasn't the most exciting.

It definitely was for me because I didn't know the score.

Florida made a free throw to take a three-point lead. Then little J.J. Jackson banked in a three-point basket at the buzzer to tie the game and send it into overtime. That's the way it was with that team, a new star almost every night and players with a lot of determination who wouldn't be denied.

The overtime was wild, back and forth, and I guess I was a nervous wreck. When the buzzer sounded, I thought the game was tied and we were headed into a second overtime. I remember the officials running off the court with me chasing them. They disappeared and, for some reason, I had the presence of mind to look at the scoreboard hanging overhead.

Wow, it said Alabama 86, Florida 85. At that point I realized why everybody was going nuts. Looking back, I'm not so sure that wasn't the most exciting game in the history of the SEC.

I've talked about our nice run through the 1987 SEC Tournament, when we beat Tennessee, 68-60, after a scrap, Auburn, 87-68, going away, and LSU, 69-62, to lock up the championship.

We had a nice seed in the NCAA Tournament that year, second in the Southeast Region, and the first two rounds were in Birmingham. We didn't consider that a payback for the fiasco the year before, but we welcomed it nonetheless. We had North Carolina A&T in the first round, an 88-71 win, and New Orleans in the second round, a 101-76 win.

Jim Farmer and Derrick McKey scored 29 points and 24 points, respectively, against North Carolina A&T. As usual, "Big D" got 14 rebounds to lead us to a good opening round victory.

As good as Derrick McKey was, which was exceptional, I never felt like I got him to play as hard as he could have. So one day I summoned him to my office and said, "Derrick, why can't I get you to go at full speed all the time. What do I need to do to help you tap your potential?" Derrick smiled and said, "Coach, it'd help if you wouldn't yell at me so much."

Well, I guess you could call that meeting a draw because I knew I couldn't coach without yelling a little bit.

The win over New Orleans came at the expense of my longtime friend and former assistant coach Benny Dees. He had a good team that season, but we were at our best that day. Derrick scored 26, Mark Gottfried scored 20, Jim scored 19 and Terry Coner scored 17. We made 40 of 55 field goal attempts, 72.7 percent, so you can tell we were on a roll.

We sat in the stands after that and watched Providence defeat Austin Peay to secure the right to play us in the next round. The Providence coach was Rick Pitino, the future Kentucky coach, and I really felt for him during that time because he and his wife had just lost a child from a totally unexpected illness.

That was a strange game because it went into overtime in an uneventful manner. An Austin Peay player had two free throws after time had expired to win the game in regulation. He missed them both.

I wasn't playing favorites while watching that day. But a week later I would've given almost anything had Austin Peay defeated Providence.

We played Providence at Freedom Hall in Louisville. They had a fine team, but they weren't fast and most people gave us an advantage. Well, they defeated us, 103-82, which was a terrible way for that Alabama team to see its season end.

Providence was led by Billy Donovan, the current Florida coach, a good one, and Delray Brooks. We couldn't slow down those two guards, particularly when they ran a three-point goal offense. They both made five treys, or 30 points that way, and one of their forwards, Ernie Lewis, made three treys.

Providence made 14 of 22 from the three-point arc. In fact, we made five of our first seven field goal attempts, a darn fine percentage, and found ourselves six or eight points behind. Rick had a Final Four club, but we scored 82 points, which should've been enough to win.

John Thompson, the Georgetown coach, had his team in Louisville, too, and after watching our loss to the Friars he said he thought we should have extended the defense to halfcourt to keep them from shooting three-point baskets. Of course, a couple nights later his Hoyas got beat by Providence.

I've second-guessed myself a million times trying to come up with something we could've done to help our defense that night. I'm still drawing a blank. With all due respect to Coach Thompson, extending the defense to stop the treys wouldn't have done it because their inside players made 19 of 26 field goal attempts. What is more, they made 23 of 30 free throws and outrebounded us, 33-23, so I guess you could call it total domination for two halves.

I guess I felt like Benny Dees did after we shot out the lights to beat New Orleans.

It was a disappointing end to a wonderful year. However, I'm still extremely proud of that team. I just wish those players could've gone farther because they sure gave me a lot of thrills during that season.

We went to work recruiting after the 1987 season with the realization the 1988 season might be a rebuilding effort because of graduation losses. Still, I felt good because Derrick McKey, Michael Ansley and Keith Askins gave us a good nucleus around which to build. I figured the addition of a good guard, maybe a junior college transfer, to go with Craig Dudley might give us enough manpower to be competitive. We got the guards, Alvin Lee, Gary Waites and Bryant Lancaster, and we added Melvin Cheatum on the inside. We were going to be young when it came to depth, but suddenly we looked deeper than I thought we would.

Little did I know what would hit me during the spring, at about the time recruiting ended.

I came in late one afternoon and Annette told me the FBI had called me and wanted to set up a meeting. Naturally, I couldn't figure out what had happened, so I telephoned them and got some terrible news. They said that while reviewing some checks in New York that were related to sports agents they had discovered a document that indicated Derrick McKey had signed with one of them and had accepted some money.

I knew the consequences of that, if it was true. Pure and simple, "Big D" would be ruled ineligible for what would be his senior season.

I remember getting in the car, going to Paul Bryant Hall and asking Derrick if he had taken any money. He said he hadn't taken any money, but I could tell he was worried about it.

Before I go any further let me say Derrick McKey is a fine person and at that time was a quiet, unassuming and polite young man. There were times when he didn't play as hard as I wanted him, too, but, boy, he could play and he never caused me any problems. I liked him very much and I still like him very much.

Derrick and I went to my office and sat down for a while. I explained to him that if he had taken money, he needed to tell me the truth. I told him the pro draft was coming up in a few weeks and I could get him entered in it and he would be drafted high and make some money. Also, I told him I didn't want him to leave if he hadn't taken money, that he meant the world to our program.

Derrick looked at me eye to eye and said, "Coach, yes, I did take some money from an agent."

That was a disappointing day, one of the really bad ones in my coaching career. We were in pretty good shape with him on the team. I knew we weren't going to be in such good shape with him playing in the NBA.

I called a friend, an agent and a confidant in New York who I knew would treat Derrick right. I explained the situation to him. Also, I told him I wanted him to take Jim Farmer, who needed an agent, and to set up Derrick and him for the draft.

After the announcement that Derrick had qualified for the NBA draft, I got calls from people with NBA teams who wanted to know if there had been a problem. I told them no, that "Big D" was a super person who was ready to turn pro.

That was devastating for us. Derrick was drafted in the first round by the Seattle SuperSonics, which made him wealthy, and Jim was drafted later in the first round by the Dallas Mavericks. Because of an error in judgment, "Big D" was gone, which meant we lost 18 points and eight rebounds per game, plus one of the finer defensive players ever in the SEC. That's a load to make up.

I must say Derrick felt bad about leaving the University of Alabama in such a pickle. In fact, he has made numerous nice financial contributions to the school since making it big in pro basketball.

I learned later that Derrick had met the agent after he had contacted Terry Coner, our super point guard in 1987, and attempted to position himself as his representative in the pro draft. Interestingly, these behind the scenes and uncalled for dealings were taking place late in the 1987 season, even as we were playing in the NCAA Tournament.

I'm not making an alibi for that loss to Providence, because that team whipped us and proved it had mettle by getting to the Final Four. Still, that Alabama team that produced the most wins in the history of the program, 28, had some distractions with which to deal, particularly going down the stretch.

So, with that in mind, I'll take a break to tell you more about the Derrick McKey case in an effort to point out how sports agents with an eye on making money can disrupt an extremely nice and somewhat naive player's life. Also, being totally honest, I think it's obvious that situation had a lingering effect on the players we had on our team the following season.

Believe me, it's difficult to lose a talent like "Big D" and keep rolling because recruiting is based on players developing in cycles and specific needs being filled year after year.

CHAPTER TWELVE

A Distressful Situation for All of Us

Terry Coner was a standout point guard for the University of Alabama

I'm sure the name Robert Potts is familiar to University of Alabama basketball fans who followed news media accounts of the Derrick McKey situation. He's the former legal counsel for the university who initiated the filing of a civil action lawsuit against Norby Walters and Lloyd Bloom, the sports agents who got "Big D" and Terry Coner to sign representation agreements with them before their collegiate eligibility had expired.

But Robert Potts, who now is president of the University of North Alabama, did much more than that. He recouped a sizeable amount of money for the Alabama Athletics Department and has been most influential in National Collegiate Athletic Association efforts to better police unscrupulous sports agents.

Robert Potts got involved in the situation when I telephoned him the day Derrick McKey admitted to me that he had accepted money from Lloyd Bloom. Like me, he knew "Big D" would be ruled ineligible by the NCAA and would have to miss his senior season at Alabama unless unusual circumstances could be determined and advanced to the NCAA Eligibility Committee. The Terry Coner case, although serious, was not as troubling because he had completed his eligibility with us.

As for me, I was thankful I didn't know anything about the involvement Derrick and Terry had with the sports agents until the FBI telephoned me on May 7, 1987. Nor did anybody else associated with our program and the University of Alabama as a whole, which meant we were in the clear as far as NCAA rules were concerned.

Also, I'm glad we moved swiftly in declaring Derrick ineligible. There are numerous cases on the books that point out the importance of reporting a possible rules infraction quickly while assuming the worse and attempting to discover the best. Again, let me point out that my athletics director during that troubling time for our basketball program was Steve Sloan, who handled the situation magnificently.

Before I get deeper into the Derrick McKey and Terry Coner cases, let me tell you more about the parties involved, specifically Norby Walters and Lloyd Bloom. Most of what I will advance I learned from an article in *Sports Illustrated* on August 3, 1987, which included the situation with "Big D" in it.

Walters was in his 60s and Bloom was in his 20s. They were involved with World Sports & Entertainment, a New York City firm that dealt with movie stars, singers, pro athletes and other entertainers. They had recently made a hard push in the representation of college athletes who were about to become pros. They worked the Southeastern Conference extensively, signing as clients, among others, Tim McGee, a Tennessee football player, Brent Fullwood, an Auburn football player, and, of course, Derrick and Terry. They signed those three players while they were still competing at the collegiate level. They did the same thing with many other college stars, hundreds I'm told, and they seemed to prey on those who were relatively poor.

At least two conferences, the SEC one of them, learned about the influence of Walters and Bloom and initiated inquiries into the performances of the players they had signed. Apparently, they wanted to see if there was any evidence of subpar efforts in an effort to rig the outcomes of games. Thank goodness, they found no such effort as it pertained to Derrick and Terry, who were a couple of players who worked hard every minute they were on the court during games.

Walters and Bloom were cornering the market as sports agents, much to the disgust of their competitors, and they became extremely miffed when many of the college stars they signed left them high and dry and secured other sports agents. Derrick was one of them who left the fold, so to speak, and apparently he made a wise decision.

Robert told me recently that Walters and Bloom were fined and sentenced to prison after being convicted of racketeering, mail fraud and conspiracy in federal court in Chicago, Illinois during the fall of 1989. Later, he said, Bloom was shot and killed on the West Coast.

I know that sounds like a movie. But that's the cast and here's the nuts of bolts of what happened, according to Robert Potts, who was more in the know than me.

On February 12, 1987, Bloom checked into the Sheraton Capstone Hotel on the University of Alabama campus. He had a travel companion, former Long Beach State football player Terry Bolar, and he sent him to contact Derrick McKey and Terry Coner and bring them to his room.

That would have been during the relatively early stages of an 11-game winning streak we had before being defeated by Providence in the Sweet 16 of the NCAA Tournament.

After Derrick and Terry arrived at the hotel, Bloom opened a briefcase stuffed with cash and said, "You need some money, don't you?"

Well, Derrick and Terry succumbed to the temptation. They accepted cash and signed contracts with World Sports & Entertainment, making Walters and Bloom their agents. They signed notes promising to repay the money after they received their bonuses for signing pro contracts.

Meanwhile, Walters and Bloom were being investigated by a federal grand jury in Chicago. When the FBI searched their offices in New York, they discovered the contracts Derrick and Terry had signed, among many others like them.

Derrick and Terry, as well as other players, had been warned about sports agents. We had a program that did that. The SEC had one. The NCAA had one. So I'm disappointed they signed those contracts, making serious errors in judgement, but I'm not mad at either one them now.

But after I got that telephone call from the FBI and Derrick confirmed he had signed with Walters and Bloom, in the words of Robert Potts, "If you think Wimp gets upset about a bad call from a referee, you ought to see him when the FBI contacts him about two of his better players."

I called Robert after meeting with Derrick. We had lunch at Paul Bryant Hall and discussed what we needed to do after contacting the NCAA and declaring "Big D" ineligible for more competition while at Alabama. We explored possible ways to get his eligibility reinstated, knowing the chances were slim, and that became more complicated.

The Seattle SuperSonics had already given Derrick $50,000 of his professional signing bonus. He spent much of that on a new car and there were no means by which to repay the money, short of a violation of a NCAA rule. What is more, the lawyer for the SuperSonics threatened to sue us if we attempted to get Derrick's eligibility restored.

Robert Potts was a rock. He didn't back down after the threat of a lawsuit. Instead, he talked with the people at the NCAA Office. Soon, it became apparent we couldn't do a thing, even if Derrick was wanting to stay at Alabama for another season.

I would never put a monetary issue in front of what is best for a young man, particularly one I was coaching, but there was a financial crisis attached to the Derrick McKey and Terry Coner case because of a NCAA rule.

The University of Alabama secured $633,616 as its share of the proceeds from the 1987 NCAA Tournament. Under SEC rules half of those proceeds went to other conference members and ten percent went to our program for expenses. However, forty percent was withheld from Alabama until a final accounting could be made by the NCAA, as is the case with everybody. That total withheld was $253,447.

NCAA regulations at that time stated that "when an ineligible student-athlete participates in a NCAA championship and the student-athlete or the institution knew or had reason to know of the ineligibility" then ninety percent of the share of the proceeds would be withheld by the NCAA executive director. That penalty was invoked against the University of Alabama.

Again, Robert Potts went to work.

Robert came up with the idea of suing Walters and Bloom in a civil action for intentional interference with a contract. The contract was the grant in aid Derrick McKey signed with the University of Alabama. It is considered a renewable contract by Alabama law, a single year agreement. The grant in aid Terry Coner signed did not come into play because it was voided because his eligibility had elapsed.

At the same time Robert was initiating the civil action against Walters and Bloom, Don Siegelman, now the Alabama governor and then the state attorney general, was pursuing Walters and Bloom on criminal charges. Part of that prosecution's strategy was the revelation the sports agents were associated with the mafia, which was later alleged in other places.

In fact, Michael Franzese, an admitted associate with the Columbo crime family, who was quoted frequently in the aforementioned *Sports Illustrated* article, made a speech at a NCAA meeting that was related to the influence of organized crime on college sports. His focus was gambling.

I don't recall all of the specifics of the civil case filed by the University of Alabama against Walters and Bloom, just that the criminal case staged in Tuscaloosa brought a lot of the national news media to campus. Also, Robert Potts recalls security being tightened in the area because of the alleged mafia ties to the two defendants.

But I do know that as the criminal case was about to begin, Walters' lawyer, Robert Gold, moved to get the civil lawsuit filed by the university settled. That happened, with Walters mandated to pay the University of Alabama $200,000.

Robert said Walters was to pay $50,000 down and $150,000 through a promissory note secured by a letter of credit from Citibank of New York. By November 16, 1989, the balance due from Walters was about $58,000.

I have no idea if the University of Alabama ever collected all of that money. But I know I felt sick because two nice young men got themselves involved in a mess.

CHAPTER THIRTEEN

The 1980s: A Decade to Remember

(Continued)

After one down season, the victories kept coming for the Alabama Crimson Tide

We attempted to put the loss of Derrick McKey behind us. But the 1988 season was horrible. We lost four nonconference games and started 0-5 in the SEC. We struggled throughout. Our record is listed in the media guide at 14-17. However, Kentucky had to forfeit two wins over us because it used an ineligible player. I don't have much pride. I'll take those games and improve our record to 16-15 because the players we had worked hard.

I won't count the forfeits in my personal record against Kentucky. However, I think our coaching staff did its best job in 1988 just trying to hold things together.

It was one and out in the SEC Tournament, which wasn't customary for Alabama. It was the only time in my 12 years as the Crimson Tide's coach when we didn't get into a postseason tournament, either the NCAA or the NIT.

It was disappointing. But I'll never forget the effort that team put forward, with Keith Askins, Michael Ansley and Craig Dudley leading the way. I guess Craig sort of epitomized the entire ordeal because he played guard like a gangbuster while wearing a heavy knee brace. I knew when the 1988 season was over there was an enormous amount of pride in Alabama basketball. That's where winning starts.

The agony of the 1988 season turned into ecstasy during the 1989 season, when we had a 23-8 record, reversed our SEC record from the year previous to 12-6 and won the SEC Tournament. It was a dramatic turnaround, like a boxer who had been floored getting off the mat to knock out an opponent.

But there was a lot more to the satisfaction than that because we rejuvenated the basketball program after the bottom fell out.

Sometimes when you're up and going places and a slide starts the slide can last for a long time. It didn't happen at Alabama, thanks to our assistant coaches recruiting well, like Kevin Gray and Greg Polinsky, and our players showing pride.

Michael Ansley was a senior and Keith Askins was a junior. They were good leaders because they had been around the block. We had just recruited David Benoit, a 6-foot-8 center, and he was a great addition. Melvin Cheatum, a 6-foot-8 forward, was a sophomore. Robert Horry was a freshman. Alvin Lee was our shooting guard, at times too much of one, and Gary Waites was a sophomore point guard who'll always be one my favorites.

I guess the high water mark that year was winning the SEC Tournament in Knoxville, Tennessee. We got by a couple of scrappy opponents in the first two rounds, 64-56 over Ole Miss and 83-79 over Vanderbilt, a fine team coached by C.M. Newton. Then we caught Florida in the finals and won, 72-60, thanks to some superb three-point shooting by Keith Askins.

Then came a game that I'd like to forget and the folks in Mobile, Alabama will talk about forever. We went to Atlanta, Georgia and had to play South Alabama in the first round of the NCAA Tournament. They beat us by two points, 86-84. It was clearly one of the most disappointing losses we had at Alabama during my time there, without question.

I had a lot of enemies in the state during that time because I refused to schedule UAB and South Alabama for regular season games. There were a lot of mad people who got fired up for that game and the news media really set the stage.

I think of all the games I coached, that was one of my poorer efforts because I didn't get our players as motivated as they should have been in the second half. We played well and got a big lead. Then we lost the lead in the second half.

I tried not to show it, but that one hurt. It was devastating because of all of the hoopla. I tried not to show how upset I was with the loss. I just congratulated South Alabama, tried to smile, although I couldn't, and went on my way.

As I said earlier, consistency is the benchmark for a winning program and I think our effort in 1990 showed we passed the test with flying colors. By the time we were finished that year, we had a 26-9 overall record and a 12-6 SEC record, good enough for second place. We added another SEC Tournament trophy to the case, our fourth in eight years, and we made another Sweet Sixteen appearance in the NCAA Tournament.

We started the season on a pleasant note, too, winning three games in the San Juan Sunshine Shootout. We beat Western Kentucky, Eastern Michigan and Clemson and, of course, enjoyed our time in Puerto Rico.

Cliff Ellis, who is coaching at Auburn now, had a fine team at Clemson that year, so that 57-48 victory was most encouraging.

In our fourth game we got an extremely pleasing win over North Carolina, 101-93, knocking off a traditional heavyweight at Coleman Coliseum in Tuscaloosa.

The game against the Tar Heels had an interesting origin. Coach Dean Smith telephoned me and asked if we had a date open, that he wanted to give one of his players, Peter Chilcutt of Tuscaloosa, the opportunity to play a game in front of his relatives and hometown friends. That was an interesting proposition because I had attempted to recruit him for Alabama. In fact, Annette and I took his mother to see Joan Rivers live at Foster Auditorium during the recruitment, which was a killer for me because I can't stand that comedian.

Dean said he wanted to make it a home and home arrangement, but that he understood if that rubbed me the wrong way after he had gotten Peter Chilcutt to sign with North Carolina. I told him, "No, I'm okay with it. Let's play a couple of games. I think playing North Carolina here will be great for our fans."

North Carolina came marching into Tuscaloosa and we sent them home with a loss.

In our next game, we got pinched at Virginia Tech, 76-75, and after three more wins we got pinched at Wake Forest, 67-65. We were off to a 7-2 start, after playing some quality teams, but I didn't think my team was playing as hard as it should have been. That led to me saying something after the loss at Wake Forest that I really regretted.

I was on the postgame radio show and said, "This is one of the lowest points of my career." I was talking about the team not playing hard. I was hacked at my players. In fact, I told David Hobbs, one of our assistant coaches, to bring the team back early from Christmas break so we can get our players' attention. But Wake Forest Coach Dave Odom, a super coach and one of my better friends, took it the wrong way. He thought I was slighting Wake Forest with that comment, saying it was a disgrace for us to lose to them, when that wasn't the point at all.

I should have chosen my words more carefully. I'm delighted Dave recently hired my son Barry as one of his assistant coaches. I guess he has forgiven me, at long last.

Anyway, I got my guys to play a little harder and we ended up having a terrific year.

The NCAA Tournament bracket sent us to Long Beach, California, where our first round opponent was Colorado State. Robert Horry had a fantastic game, scoring 27 points in 35 minutes, and James Sanders scored 18. I was really pleased for him because he was a walkon player, maybe the best we had at Alabama.

We faced a super challenge in the second round, Arizona, and it was unbelievable how we took apart an outstanding basketball team. The final score was 77-55, with David Benoit leading us with 20 points. Our guys really played that day. We suffocated them with our defense. We had five scorers in double figures, great balance.

I'm not sure Coach Lute Olsen's players were as motivated as they should've been. I think they might have taken us for granted.

Regardless, I exited that victory thinking we might have a team that could make it to the Final Four. We seemed to be hitting our stride at precisely the proper time.

Then came a major letdown.

I've tried not to second guess myself, choosing to take a loss hard and put it aside, if possible. Maybe I shouldn't second guess myself now while looking back on the loss we had to Loyola-Marymount in our next game. I'll just give you the specifics and let you be the judge.

The game was in Oakland, California. You'll remember Loyola-Marymount had lost Hank Gaithers, who had died, and they had dedicated the season to him. In fact, one of their players shot a free throw lefthanded in the game in honor of his fallen teammate.

Loyola-Marymount had been averaging more than 100 points per game. That team was the toast of the nation, at least one of them, and we had to battle that.

We stayed in California to prepare because it would've been foolish to waste what would have amounted to a couple of days traveling home and turning around and traveling back to the West Coast. We worked out at Long Beach State.

During the week leading up to the game, I called every coach I knew whose team had played Loyola-Marymount in an effort to figure out how to slow them down. Each said something like this: "Wimp, you might think your team can run with that team. But you can't. If you get in a running match with Loyola-Marymount in a one-game series like this, you're going to get beat. I know you think you've got better players and maybe you do. But you're not going to outrun them."

I really struggled with that game plan. I had a team that had been in the 60s and 70s most of the year and had won with defense. But Loyola-Marymount wasn't known as one of the truly great defensive teams in history, either, so it was a hard call.

I decided to milk the shot clock on almost every possession, to slow the pace to a point where we were comfortable. We felt like we'd get good shots.

Paul Westhead was their coach and he was a darn fine one. We went to dinner the night before the game and had an enjoyable time.

Well, we fell behind 9-2 in the early part of the game, which really added to my quandary. I called my team together for a timeout and there were some fans behind our bench that really started giving me the devil about the strategy we had used. I didn't say anything to them, but I was thinking they might be right.

However, I told our players we're sticking with this game plan. I don't think I've ever had a team that played as close to exactly the way I told it to play as that one did that day.

We turned the ball over a couple of times to their press in critical situations, which really hurt us. We got a bad break when Paul got into it with an official at halftime and the official walked away instead of giving him a technical foul, which he said he was about to get.

The final score was Loyola-Marymount 62, Alabama 60, a crushing defeat. They attempted 74 field goals, an unbelievable total, and we attempted 51. They beat us with their three-point shots, seven to our one.

After the game I went into a press conference and explained that our strategy wasn't designed to keep the game close or to hold Loyola-Marymount to 40 points under its average. I told the news media we had played that way in an effort to win, which we didn't, and that was that.

Richard Williams, the former Mississippi State coach and my dear friend, told me I had made a mistake, that I had the players to beat Loyola-Marymount in an higher paced game. Jerry Tarkanian, the former Nevada-Las Vegas coach who was at the game, told me the same thing.

Isn't it amazing that a decade after the fact, even with all the winning we had done, averaging about 22 wins per season, I'm still fretting over that loss in the NCAA Tournament?

CHAPTER FOURTEEN

Recruiting: Wild and Funny Stories

Part II

Wimp Sanderson remembers Alvin Lee getting a
championship ring in Knoxville, Tennessee

Certainly you know by now there were some basketball players who caused headaches for me during my years at the University of Alabama. That's the nature of the coaching business, as well as life in general.

Given his success as a professional player and the nationally known problems he has had, it might surprise some folks to learn Latrell Spreewell wasn't one of those guys. A 6-foot-5 forward for us in 1991 and 1992, now a superstar with the New York Knicks, he came to us from Three Rivers Junior College and had an excellent work ethic the entire time he was in our program.

Most people know the story about Latrell being suspended from the NBA for allegedly choking his coach. Well, when that happened a few years ago I received telephone calls from people across the nation wanting to know what type person he was while at Alabama. *People Magazine* called, *Sports Illustrated* called, *Good Morning, America* called and on and on. They wanted to get a feel for how he acted while playing for me.

I made it clear to them that I don't condone what Latrell did and I hate that happened to him. But as far as his time with us, those two years, he worked extremely hard to be the best basketball player he could be. I only had one problem with him. He was late for the team bus down in Baton Rouge, Louisiana and I held him out of the starting lineup.

What I remember most about "Spree" was that long after practices ended he would still be on the court working on his game.

Maybe money has changed "Spree" some, as has been the case with a lot of players. I know he has that tough look on his face and he has his hair braided. But I think it's still true that he plays hard, really gets after it.

We took a chance on "Spree" because of his grades and I commend Kevin Gray for getting in there during the recruiting process and working hard. We got him to campus, he worked his fanny off in summer school to get eligible and he became a terrific player on two teams I'll discuss in a future chapter.

Now let me tell you about the recruitment of some players on teams I've already talked about, starting with that super group we had in 1987.

The first time I saw Derrick McKey was strange because I really questioned what I was doing in Meridian, Mississippi. Art Tolis, one of our assistant coaches, had seen him play and told me he was a real talent, that we might have a chance to get him because his mother seemed to like us.

They were starting practice in his high school gym and Derrick was sitting on the top row of the bleachers in his sweatsuit. Lo and behold, he had his head between his legs as if he was asleep. When he eventually came down to the floor, I don't think he said five words to us. But it didn't take me long watching him work out to know he was going to make somebody a fine player.

I almost messed up his recruitment right off the bat by mentioning we might redshirt him a year and let him mature a little. I could tell that idea didn't settle too well with him and I immediately forgot that approach.

Derrick was only an hour and a half from Tuscaloosa, but he spent a lot of time in Oxford, Mississippi being recruited by Ole Miss. Stan Torgenson, the Ole Miss radio announcer, lived in Meridian and he would give Derrick rides back and forth so he could go to all of the Rebels' games he wanted.

Ultimately, we got Derrick, I think because of our winning ways at the time while Ole Miss was a little down. We beat Louisville for him, too, and that had to have been for another reason because the Cardinals had just won or were about to win a national championship.

It's interesting that Mark Gottfried, the Alabama coach now, was a tough person to recruit. He was from Mobile, Alabama and wanted to go to Oral Roberts because he liked the coach out there. I had lunch with him and his father and couldn't convince them he needed to be in Tuscaloosa. Maybe they didn't like me all that much.

Mark went to Oral Roberts in the fall of 1983, played one year and discovered the coach he liked so much was leaving the program. I went out and visited him and explained we still wanted him if he wanted to transfer. He chose to do that, even while knowing he would have to sit out the 1984 season as a redshirt.

For as long as I live I'll never forget signing Mark Gottfried to a grant in aid on the top of a taxi cab just before he had to go to class at Oral Roberts. I doubt he'll forget that since it isn't probable he would be Alabama's coach now if he hadn't joined the program then.

Our recruitment of Jim Farmer out of Dothan, Alabama in 1983 made a few of the so called experts raise their eyebrows. I thought he had some potential, although he played in a weak private school league and shot the basketball every time he touched it. Frankly, we didn't know whether to offer him a grant in aid. He was solidly built, but a little skinny, and had he not been such a pleasant person, I'm not sure we would have taken the chance.

Finally, Leroy McClendon came in my office and said, "Coach, we've got one scholarship left. Let's give it to Jim and see what he can do."

Jim went through a redshirt year, hit the weight room with a vengeance and started developing into a hulk. Ultimately, he lettered for us four years and became the 20th pick in the 1987 NBA Draft. To this day he likes to tell a story about how he would've never played at Alabama had not one of our forwards gotten hurt. Truthfully, we liked his competitive spirit when we recruited him and made the right decision to sign him. He's a good friend now and we were lucky to have him.

Now, here's a saga of a coach and a player that still makes me smile, the story of Wimp Sanderson and Michael Ansley.

Michael, who played forward for us from 1986 through 1989, was another guy I recruited mighty hard. He turned out to be one of the better shooters we had at Alabama, but he was also a fly by night sort of person who didn't care much about going to school. There were times when he really had to be pushed.

I was in Nashville playing in a golf tournament not long after we signed Michael. This was during the summer of 1986, when I got a telephone call from one of the assistant coaches who said Michael Ansley has gone home. I almost fainted. We had recruited a super prospect and he had bailed out before even getting enrolled in classes.

I called one of his high school coaches, who got in touch with him and helped us get Michael back to Tuscaloosa.

That brings to mind an enlightening story that involved Michael and Keith Askins, whose recruitment I'll discuss next.

During the 1989 season Michael was a senior and Keith was a junior. They were pretty good leaders and I wanted to give them some responsibility, as I attempted to do with a lot of players through the years. So I told Keith to make the curfew check that night to make sure everybody got in on time.

Well, the next morning I ran into Keith and said, "So did everybody make bed check?" He looked at me and said, "No sir. Michael Ansley was 30 minutes late."

That shows you what kind of character Keith had, particularly since Michael wanted to destroy him — and, believe me, Ansley was the kind of brawny guy who could do that to a skinny guy like Askins.

I'll tell you more about Michael, a funny memory.

We were playing in the NCAA Tournament one year and I was

practicing the team real hard. So Michael came over to me and said, "Coach, you're working us so hard we're going to boycott." I think he expected me to roll over and back off. Instead, I said, "Okay, Michael, so tell me when you're planning to leave so I can get somebody to take your place." He laughed, trotted off and went back to work.

Michael was a different type bird, for sure, but he was a good player, too. I enjoyed coaching him, all of the challenges understood. I'm proud he got to play a few years in the NBA after being drafted in the second round in 1989.

Now, back to Keith Askins, a young man who as a high school player was skin and bones and wasn't highly recruited until he put on a show in the first game of the high school state tournament.

I got a call from a high school coach in Athens, Alabama who said they thought Keith had a chance to be a fine player. I went up there to see him in the last game of the season. He didn't play particularly well that night, but I thought he had terrific potential. I know the alums I was with thought I was crazy.

I invited Keith to come down for a visit. I believe it was during the week of the high school state tournament. He said, "Coach, thank you, I'll be there. You've got my word."

Keith played great in the first round of the state tournament and college coaches were lined up outside the dressing room wanting to talk to him. He never wavered. He stuck with his commitment. He was a great player for us.

I'm extremely happy for Keith because he made a good run with the Miami Heat in the NBA, playing a full decade. That's pretty good for a guy who at one point nobody wanted except me.

I'm going back to the 1970s to catch up on some recruiting stories I missed a few chapters ago.

The first involved Raymond Odums, a lightning quick guard for us from 1972 through 1974 and one of the earlier minority players we had in the Alabama program. One year earlier we had successfully recruited Wendell Hudson, so it wasn't hard for us to follow with Raymond Odums, who was a splendid athlete, as good in football as he was basketball.

Our problem was containing his speed, which led to a bewildering experience at practice during his first season.

The players were about to run wind sprints and Coach C.M. Newton said he didn't think we should let Raymond run because he might crash into the brick wall at the end of the court. I told C.M. that was ridiculous, that he needed to run.

Well, sure enough, he was moving so fast he hit the wall before he could stop and busted out several teeth. I felt terrible about that the whole time he was there.

If C.M. was frightened watching Raymond Odums crash into the wall, I was literally terrified one evening during the 1970s while recruiting a player nicknamed "Banana" at Carver High School. I went up there to see him and remember there were a bunch of kids in the streets having a balloon fight.

Well, I made the visit and went to my car to leave. Then I discovered I had locked my keys inside. So I had to go back inside, borrow a coat hangar and try to open the car door with it.

Race relations in Alabama weren't as good then as they are now, although they were improving significantly, maybe in part because of our recruiting policies. Suffice it to say, it wasn't comfortable being the only white person within miles trying to open a car door with a coat hangar with those folks watching me.

I've talked about winning more than a few recruiting battles with Auburn, as well as a few I lost. But I really almost dropped the ball trying to land Mike Davis, a terrific guard from Fayette County High School who would be a standout for Alabama from 1980 through 1983.

I spent night and day trying to get him to sign. Herman Williams was recruiting him for Auburn and I got up after several visits thinking I had lost him to my buddy Sonny Smith.

However, I kept going back to Fayette and after Mike signed with us, his mother, an extremely nice lady, said every time she tossed out the dish water she would see Wimp Sanderson or Herman Williams in the back yard.

As of this writing, Mike is coaching on Bobby Knight's staff at Indiana, which brings to mind how much his boss wanted him to play for him in 1980 through 1983. In fact, Bobby had a strong interest in several of our players, most notably T.R. Dunn, Reggie King and Mike. Through the years he has spent time talking about how exceptional those three were as players and individuals.

I've saved my reflections on the recruiting and coaching of a couple of guys for last because they're extremely special to me. I think you'll be surprised to hear their names because Gary Waites, a 6-foot-2 guard for us from 1988 through 1991, and Alvin Lee, a 6-foot-1 guard for us in 1988 and 1989, aren't two guys who easily come to mind among Crimson Tide fans.

I guess Gary has to be one of my favorites because he worked hard, had terrible knee surgery and kept plowing until he was finished.

I was in Atlanta, Georgia with Greg Polinsky, one of my assistant coaches, watching a summer basketball camp. We had been over there all day and I was worn out and ready to go home.

Greg said, "Coach, I want you to watch one more game. They've got a guy in this one who is really quick. We need to take a hard look." I said, "Okay, we'll take a peek and then go home."

Well, when Gary got on the court he was quicker than a hiccup — really, really, really fast and very, very, very good. I watched him like a hawk.

At halftime, Gary went out into the hallway of the auditorium to get a drink of water. I was on his heels, moving about like he did on the court.

There were two water fountains side by side. When he bent

over to get a slurp of water out of one, I bent over to get a slurp of water out the other one. In the process of slurping, I said, "Gary, Coach Sanderson from Alabama. We'll be in contact with you."

After that strange and wet introduction, Greg and I worked hard on Gary Waites. I was delighted when we signed him.

To this day, Gary Waites is as hardnosed a point guard as you'll ever find. He worked through his injury and got well quicker than anybody I've seen. He played on Alabama teams that won 86 games, 72 during his sophomore, junior and senior years. Not only that, he was a delight to be around and a delight to coach.

Now for Alvin Lee, who I can't talk about much without getting emotional.

Alvin was a guy we couldn't handle after recruiting him out of a junior college. He was selfish. He didn't want to play for the team. He wanted to shoot the basketball all of the time. He didn't want to play defense, not one iota.

When I'd go into staff meetings, it was four-to-one that we should get rid of Alvin Lee because he was such a liability to the team. I was the one. Fortunately, I was the boss. I decided to hang with the guy, for a reason beyond me, and I did.

Eventually, Alvin became a hard worker and real team player. He contributed mightily to our 23-8 record in 1989. He and I became close. I think he appreciated the University of Alabama sticking with him. I know I appreciated the turnaround he made on the court and in life in general.

So comes to mind a story about Alvin Lee and what he did during the 1989 Southeastern Conference Tournament in Knoxville, Tennessee. This was just prior to the championship game against Florida, after we had beaten Ole Miss and Vanderbilt in the first two rounds.

We broke the huddle to run out for the opening tip. Just before the officials were ready to toss the basketball into the air, Alvin ran back to our bench. He took a hand and rubbed the SEC championship ring I was wearing. Then he grinned, ran back out there and played super while winning one for himself.

Last year, in 1999, Alvin Lee was killed in an automobile accident. I'm still remorseful. Also, I'm still thankful for what he did for Alabama basketball and for me as his coach.

That's the way it is for a coach, at least for me. You can't lose sight of who does the winning, the players, and, believe me, I had my share of outstanding young men on my teams.

CHAPTER FIFTEEN

Watching the Children Grow Up Quickly

Annette Sanderson was a knowledgeable and supportive University of Alabama basketball fan as the first lady of the Crimson Tide program

As is the case with most people, I guess, the year 1990 was a time of reflection for the Sanderson family. That tends to happen when decades change.

Annette and I had been married for more than 30 years. We had lived in Tuscaloosa, Alabama for almost three decades, in a rented house in Abrams Place, in a great little red brick house on 15th Street, in a more spacious house we built in Woodland Hills and in a comfortable house we built on the golf course at NorthRiver Yacht Club.

I had always wanted to live on a golf course and that's where we were when the 1990s rolled around.

Annette had her group of closely knit friends and I had mine. We remained a private family, with me consumed by basketball, and the quiet time by ourselves was grand.

The boys, Jim, Scott and Barry, were pretty much grown and on their own, although we stayed in close contact. All of them displayed a strong interest in basketball as children, as well as in coaching as they grew older, and, quietly, that pleased me. I'll admit I tried to discourage them a little bit because of the demands of the occupation. That might've been my way to make sure they knew what they were getting into.

They must not have believed what I was telling them because Jim, Scott and Barry are coaching college basketball now — and their father is smiling.

I'm going to tell you about those fine men at this point in the book because as I'm writing it Annette and I are awaiting the arrival of our eighth grandchild.

You might remember all three of my sons got their baptisms

in basketball playing hot tail with me, as I had playing the game with older boys in Florence, Alabama. So that's where I'll start telling you about their remarkable journeys in the sport, beginning in the mid-1970s, when Jim was playing at Eastwood Junior High School in Tuscaloosa, Scott was at Arcadia Elementary School and Barry was about to start school and was getting better at hot tail while playing with me in Woodland Hills.

Being the oldest, Jim was the first of our children to get into organized basketball and I really enjoyed watching him play at Eastwood Junior High School. It took me back to my years as a frail kid when I tried to get started in the sport.

Jim played basketball at Central High School in Tuscaloosa, which meant I got to watch him, and he did well enough to go on to Brewer State Junior College in Fayette, Alabama. He got an apartment up there and continued his basketball playing career.

Wanting to continue his playing career, Jim went to the University of North Alabama and, more or less, tried out for the team. He decided he wouldn't be able to play much, so he returned to Tuscaloosa, got his degree and started his coaching career at Curry High School. All of that was extremely interesting because I had gone to Florence State Teachers College, which became UNA, and I had started coaching in Carbon Hill, which about the distance of a free throw from Curry High School.

After two seasons at Curry High School, in 1985 Jim got the opportunity to coach at Faulkner University in Montgomery. He stayed there four years, then went to Western Carolina as an assistant coach for one season.

From 1990 through 1994, Jim coached at Guntersville High School. Interestingly, at that time he was asked to return to Faulkner University and he's coaching there at this time.

Jim is married, is a model citizen and, in my opinion, is an excellent coach. He and his wife, Jill, have two children, Katie and Kyle.

Scott played basketball for a good coach at Central High School in Tuscaloosa, Roosevelt Sanders, and he was able to attend several summer camps. A lot of college coaches were looking for players and Ray Jones, who was at Furman University at the time, took a serious interest in him. So did Richmond and a couple of other programs.

Scott liked Furman and was ready to sign a scholarship to play there. But Ray Jones, the coach who had recruited him, made a move to South Carolina to work for Bill Foster, a super coach.

I was in Arizona at a basketball camp when Scott telephoned me and said he had committed to Furman but he thought South Carolina was going to offer him a scholarship. He wanted me to tell him what to do, so I suggested he visit South Carolina and see what he thought about that school. Honestly, I thought it was a great school and a good program and he would get the chance to play there.

Scott chose to go to South Carolina and I don't think he has regretted the decision. He played four years under Bill Foster, got to travel all over the country and made some great friends.

After Scott graduated at South Carolina, he was a graduate assistant coach there for one season. The next year, Jim hired him as an assistant coach at Faulkner University, where he stayed two years, 1986 and 1987. You can imagine I was as proud as a peacock watching my two oldest boys working together.

I was visiting one day with Dave Odom, my good friend, who had just become an assistant coach at Virginia under Terry Holland. I asked if he thought there was a chance Scott might have an opportunity to work with them. They hired him and he learned a lot in one season.

Then Scott got a great break, an opening on the staff of Tim Floyd at New Orleans. I had known Tim since he was an assistant coach at Texas El Paso and thought the world of him.

In fact, during those years Tim would telephone me and ask what players we were recruiting in Alabama, that he might want to come into the state and go after the ones we weren't trying to sign. That shows how good he was as a recruiter.

Anyway, I contacted Tim and told him where Scott had been and asked if he was willing to interview him. That's called networking, with a family touch, and it worked wonders. In fact, Tim said an interview wasn't needed, that if Scott was my son he had a job at New Orleans.

Scott learned a ton from Tim Floyd, for whom he worked three seasons, and they're still super friends who frequently talk on the telephone and get together for visits in Nashville.

In 1990, Joe Harrington, another of my friends, became coach at Colorado. We were in Denver for the NCAA Tournament, so I found Joe and asked if he would be interested in hiring Scott as an assistant coach. They got together, really hit it off and worked together until 1996.

Joe resigned that year, actually with games remaining to be played, and Scott was hopeful he would become the head coach. That wasn't in the cards, so he attempted to become the head coach at Mobile College, where former Auburn football coach Doug Barfield was the athletics director.

Doug hired Scott, which provided him with a great opportunity. He did extremely well in three seasons, once taking his team to the NAIA national championship game in Tulsa, Oklahoma, where Mobile College lost to Life College.

Last year, in 1999, Scott was hired as coach at David Lipscomb University in Nashville, Tennessee. His first team made it to the final eight of the NAIA Tournament and now he will lead that program as it moves to the NCAA Division I level.

Now, please lend an ear to this.

Last year, Jim's team at Faulkner University really overachieved, which is a credit to him, and it advanced to the final eight of the NAIA Tournament. If his team and Scott's team had been able to secure one more victory each they would have coached against each other in the national semifinals.

I was hopeful it would happen because a father wants to see his sons have success. On the other hand, Annette and I weren't looking forward to watching them compete against each other.

Scott and his wife, Ronda, have three sons, Carter, Clint and Garrett. Another son is on the way.

Barry was smaller than Jim and Scott, but he enjoyed playing, too, and did fine at Central High School. Then he enrolled at Alabama and spent a lot of time around our team and our assistant coaches. That was a blessing for me, really enjoyable, because, as most parents agree, there's something bewildering about the youngest child leaving the fold.

The experience made Barry more interesting in becoming a coach and he was able to spend a year working under Kermit Davis Jr. at Texas A&M. After that, he moved to Georgia as a graduate assistant coach under Hugh Durham, which really pleased me because we're such good friends and he's such an exceptional coach.

It's interesting that the next place Barry coached was Arkansas-Little Rock, where I'd end up going after my departure from Alabama. In fact, he worked with me in Little Rock before going to East Carolina for one year.

In keeping with what seems like a family tradition, at least strong ties, Barry was coaching on Scott's staff at David

Lipscomb in Nashville. Now he's moving on to Wake Forest.

Barry and his wife, Kristen, have two children, Caroline and Blake.

All three of my sons seemed to want to coach basketball, maybe because that's all I've ever done and they've been around it all of their lives.

I'm delighted with all of them.

Jim, Scott and Barry have always done things a little differently and that's the case with their approaches to coaching. They handle players and situations differently, as they should, and they've done excellent jobs.

More importantly, they're outstanding husbands and super daddies, which makes Annette and me double proud.

Similarly, Annette and I are thankful for the wonderful friendships we developed in Tuscaloosa during our three decades plus in that city. By the time we had moved to NorthRiver Yacht Club, we had what seemed like a million of them and to say life was grand is an understatement.

I was particularly excited about the move to NorthRiver Yacht Club, a beautiful area about fifteen minutes by car from the University of Alabama campus. I got the opportunity in a weird manner, basically because for several years I liked to play softball for the Lutheran Church team.

We had a lady whose husband played on the softball team and, basically, ran the softball team. He owned a nice lot at NorthRiver Yacht Club. When he died, his wife, Aileene Dahlke, decided she wanted to sell the land instead of building a house on it, as they had planned.

So I got my buddy Harry Cole, the real estate executive I mentioned earlier, to talk with her about us buying the lot.

Our house was built on the 10th hole, in the dogleg, and I really enjoyed that. I could get home in the afternoon and walk a few holes or go down to the practice range and hit balls. It was a super way to relax after the rigors of coaching basketball and dealing with all manner of change in the Alabama Athletics Department.

As a bonus, *Golf Digest* had its famous teaching school there. Bob Toski used to teach there. So did Peter Kostas and Jim Fleck. Also, Davis Love was an instructor before he died. They were willing to give me some lessons to help my game and during that time several PGA Tour players would sneak in and out of NorthRiver to get private lessons from those greats.

To this day, I take what seems like a thousand lessons a week and still can't master that sport. But I was able to get in a few groups and played a lot of enjoyable rounds at NorthRiver Yacht Club, where there seems to be more sand than on a beach.

I had played golf previously at Tuscaloosa Country Club, where Harry Cole, Dick Zeanah, Bill McGuire, Bo Boschung and I had some great times. Also, we played gin rummy one night every week at Harry's office, with Henry "Sang" Lyda and Ray Moore joining us. Goodness, how I miss those card games and seeing those guys on a weekly basis.

We made a lot of golfing trips together, too, like one year during a fall when we went to Willow Point near Alexander City, Alabama to play. I think Alabama was playing Georgia Tech in football that weekend. We got in nine holes and hurried back to the condo to watch the game.

Bo Boschung is a professor at Alabama and Dick Zeanah owns Alabama Book Store on campus. Bill McGuire is into real estate development. We had a spirited crew and everybody was fair game when it came to ridicule and my ol' buddy Harry usually got more than his share.

There was a kickoff that went out of bounds in the game and Harry was surprised when they put the football in play without making the kicking team kick again. He didn't know the new rule and that really bothered him.

Well, we were discussing every play. At one point, Bo and Dick started arguing about whether Alabama should have kicked a field goal. I let them go at it for a few minutes and then got involved.

I told them the reason Alabama didn't kick a field goal at that point in the game was a new rule that had been put in place that season, the opportunity to try for a four-point field goal in the fourth quarter. Well, Harry didn't say a thing. He just sat and listened with his eyes glued on the television set. Meanwhile, the other guys really picked up on it and started talking about how a team got a four-point field goal.

After the game ended, we went back to the golf course to play the back nine. Harry forgot his cooler and went back to the condo to get it while we waited on the tee. He was gone quite a while and we got a good laugh after asking him what took so long.

Harry said he had come up on a group that was arguing over whether Alabama should have kicked a field goal. So, he said he explained the new four-point field goal rule to them.

Harry was as proud as a peacock until we told them there wasn't a four-point field goal rule. He played terrible through nine holes, obviously embarrassed, and after the round ended he found the guys he had talked to and told them he was only kidding when he told them about the new rule.

Those were some great days. As I said, Harry, has passed away and I miss him. Bo, Bill, Dick and Ray are still in Tuscaloosa. "Sang" Lyda, who was our basketball trainer and one of my chief confidants, has retired and is living in Orange Beach, Alabama.

Annette and I are living in Birmingham now, having just built a house, and we're in the process of renewing some timetested friendships and building some new ones.

As I've stated, my wife meets people easily and she has an army of friends from the times we've live in various cities, from Florence, to Tuscaloosa and to Little Rock. I've got a smaller brigade that's growing each day, in no small part because of the Sonny and Wimp Radio Show my pal Sonny Smith and I host weekday mornings.

CHAPTER SIXTEEN

1991 and 1992: Going Up — and Down

Robert Horry, a NBA championship player, was one of many Crimson Tide standouts who advanced to pro basketball

Basketball fans came early and in droves to watch our University of Alabama teams play during the mid-1980s and early 1990s. Coleman Coliseum, formerly Memorial Coliseum, was a happening place. Opposing teams marked visits to Tuscaloosa, Alabama on their calendars, sort of like we once did when putting a circle around Kentucky, Tennessee, Vanderbilt and LSU.

We had a great atmosphere for games, thanks to all of the winning some super players had done. The playing surface was parquet, supposedly as a tribute to our success, a special type home floor. Some of our supporters, particularly the students, had fans and masks that had my picture on them, the scowling face. I got a kick out of that, at least to some extent, but was concerned too much hype was being directed at me and not enough attention was being afforded my players.

I would have stopped some of the fanfare had it not been for the excitement surrounding the program. At last, we had the type support we had wanted for years.

As I've said, winning players make winning coaches and we entered the 1991 season with some troopers. Melvin Cheatum, Latrell Spreewell and Robert Horry were powers inside. My little guard who was as tough as steel, Gary Waites, was a senior. Bryant Lancaster was a guard. James "Hollywood" Robinson and Marcus Webb provided quality depth on the outside and inside, respectively.

That was a fine array of talent, one of the better groups in Alabama basketball history, and it blended good enough to produce a 23-10 record and to make another trip to the NCAA

Tournament Sweet Sixteen. That came after we lost three of our first five games, which means those guys had heart.

The 1991 team gave us one of our more pleasing victories and in the process proved you can teach an old dog new tricks. I was the mongrel in this case and the lesson I learned had come when we lost that 1989 NCAA Tournament game to South Alabama because we didn't play well in the second half.

But here's what happened in 1991.

As most people know, Robert Horry and I had our moments when we didn't see eye to eye. He was an exceptional player, a bright guy, but I had a hard time getting him to practice as hard as he played. I saw his potential. I pushed him to get him there.

Just before our final regular season game, a 96-88 win over Tennessee, it came to my attention that Robert had been doing a lot of talking about how he didn't like playing for me. I had been down that road during my first season with Eddie Phillips and I wasn't going to let this one get out of control. Robert did something that upset me during that game and I called him into the coaches' dressing room after we beat the Vols and let him have it pretty good. Maybe the timing was bad, I don't know, but he sort of sulked up and left in a huff.

We had the Southeastern Conference Tournament in front of us, that year in Nashville, Tennessee, and the next day I called Robert in for a meeting in my office.

I said, "Robert, it's my understanding you won't be back at Alabama next season if I'm the coach."

Robert said, "Yeah, that's right."

I said, "Well, Robert, you're not going to play against Florida in the first round of the SEC Tournament. You're suspended until I tell you otherwise."

A lot of the players got upset because of the suspension. Frankly, I didn't know how long the suspension would last, how many games, but I knew I was going to hold Robert out in an effort to get his attitude a little better. He was a junior who should've displayed more maturity.

Anyway, we opened the tournament without Robert against Florida, a fine team coached by Lon Kruger. At halftime we were behind 17 points. We were in a mess and I didn't know exactly what to tell our players. We hadn't played well at all in the first half. The effort might have been there, but was sketchy if it was. The Gators had the crowd behind them because of all of the success we had experienced in the SEC Tournament. It wasn't a good situation at all.

I wrote one word on the chalkboard in the dressing room at halftime: w-o-r-k. I appealed to them to work, that we could claw our way back into the game. I asked them to get back into the groove, play like Alabama was supposed to perform in the SEC Tournament.

I knew our secret to success in the tournament had been our ability to beat the teams we were supposed to beat and then see what happens in the semifinals or finals, when the matches were more even. So I told our players to work, work and work. I told them I'd work hard, too, and I prodded them until I saw some enthusiasm.

I got into the game better. We tried to make it a positive challenge. By golly, our players did get after it. They fought hard. We got back in it, like we said we could, and we beat Florida, 71-65, in a memorable game.

We beat Auburn, 77-59, in the semifinals. The Tigers were coached by Tommy Joe Eagles at that time.

Later, Phillip Pearson, a member of that team and an Alabama assistant coach now, said our players were placing bets on how long it would be before I got Robert Horry on the court when we faced Auburn. It didn't take long.

In the finals we faced Tennessee, in its home state, and the morning before the game I read something interesting in the newspaper. Wade Houston was their coach and Allen Houston, his son, was their star player. There was a quote from the son in the article I read. He said, "Oh no, I hate to play Alabama again because they're always in your face."

I used that to our advantage. I said, he's right about that. We're going to get after it, get in their faces and keep the pressure on.

We won that game, 88-69, and capped what after a hard start was a fairly easy run through the SEC Tournament.

Of course, Robert Horry was securely back in the fold by then and I think that experience helped him. He has gone on to play well as a pro, to star in the NBA Playoffs while in Houston. In fact, he's with the Los Angeles Lakers now and they're in the championship series as these words are being written. His mother has said the suspension made a positive impact. I think Robert believes that.

We were the number four seed in the NCAA Tournament Southeast Regional and opened it in Atlanta, Georgia with a 89-79 victory over Murray State. They were coached by my friend Steve Newton.

I don't know if we've had a better opening round game in a NCAA Tournament. The margin of victory wasn't that much, but we ran the court well and we shot well. Melvin Cheatum led us in scoring with 23 points and he made 11 of 15 field goal attempts. He and "Spree" led us in rebounding with nine. Robert Horry scored 21. "Hollywood" Robinson scored 15.

One of our victories early in the 1991 season was against Wake Forest, 96-95 in overtime, and that's who we had to play in the second round at The Omni.

That was an interesting matchup because of the friendship Dave Odom and I have. When he coached for Terry Holland at Virginia, they were nice enough to hire my son Scott so he could launch his coaching career. I had attempted to return the favor by hiring Dave's son Lane, who was on our staff when we played Wake Forest in the NCAA Tournament.

I know it was difficult for Lane to coach against his dad when the stakes were so high — and we won, 89-88, in what might have been the best game in the NCAA Tournament that year.

The game went back and forth and we were fortunate to win. I guess balance was the key because Gary Waites, Melvin Cheatum and "Spree" all scored 21 points, Robert Horry scored 16 and "Hollywood" scored 15. We got the margin of victory at the free throw line, making eight more than the Demon Deacons.

I don't like to think much about the next game we had in the NCAA Tournament, for good reason. Arkansas killed us, 93-70, in Charlotte, North Carolina and it remains a blur. Obviously, we didn't play much defense in that game.

Although we're good friends now, Arkansas Coach Nolan Richardson and I were feuding a little in those days because I felt like he had run up the score on one of my teams in a game a few years earlier in Little Rock. Specifically, I thought he had pressed from daylight to darkness. I said something to him after they had routed us and he said he had pressed for a reason. Well, I shouldn't have said anything because it was his team and his players were working hard that night.

Anyway, he had a fine team at his disposal. They had been to the Final Four the year before. In 1991, they produced a 34-4 record overall and a 15-1 Southwest Conference regular season record. We had a tough NCAA Tournament assignment.

There was a lot of interest in our matchup with Arkansas because that program was one year away from joining the SEC. I don't guess we put too much fear in them that night.

But Alabama won two out of three meetings with Arkansas in 1992, all barnburners, and Crimson Tide fans delighted in that semblance of revenge.

To say the 1992 season started with a bang and ended with a bang is an understatement. Actually, there was a double bang at the end because, little did I know, that was the last year I was to coach Alabama basketball.

We got a fast start on a 26-9 record in 1992 by winning eight of nine games prior to the Rainbow Classic in Honolulu, Hawaii. We added three more wins out there to claim the championship, beating Bradley, Villanova and Washington State. We had a couple of tough stretches, losing three SEC games in a row at one point and three out of five at another point. Obviously, we had long runs of success, too.

I guess the series we played with Arkansas that year was the highlight. I've had a lot of people from inside and outside our program say those three games might have been the best in history between two conference opponents in one season. Without question, they were three wild games played between two teams who had a lot of talent and worked their fannies off on both ends of the court.

We won the first meeting with Arkansas, 65-63, in Tuscaloosa. Don Rutledge, a super official, called a charging foul on them near the end and, after we were fouled during our offensive possession, we knocked down two free throws to get the victory.

We weren't that fortunate in Fayetteville, Arkansas, where we lost, 90-87, in no small measure because of me. I got a technical foul in that game that really hurt my team. I think I apologized to my players for that.

Then came the third game against Arkansas, which might be the game modern day Crimson Tide fans talk about more than all others. It came in the semifinals of the SEC Tournament, after we had won a hardfought game over Florida, 62-60, in the first round.

With 48 seconds remaining, Arkansas had a four-point lead, 89-85. Then Latrell Spreewell took the basketball, drove it into the lane and hit a short jump shot to cut it to two points.

When Arkansas got the basketball down the court, we waited for them to get the ball in the right pair of hands and fouled the man we wanted to shoot free throws. He missed the first one and we got the rebound, moved up the court and called a timeout.

I don't guess there were five seconds left, probably something like four.

We had two guards on the court, "Hollywood" Robinson, who loved to shoot three-point baskets, and Elliot Washington, an obscure guard who didn't like to shoot much at all from any range. He was a good shooter. He just didn't care to.

During the timeout, I told them what I wanted them to do. But, honestly, when we broke the huddle I think three of them thought we were going to try one thing and two of them thought we were going to try something else. It'd be interesting to ask them someday.

Anyway, we needed two points to force an overtime, which we would have accepted, and we needed three points to win, which we welcomed.

James Robinson got the basketball and I would have bet he was going to shoot. Most of the time, he wouldn't pass to his mother if she was wide open for a layup and wanted to make a basket. But, lo and behold, he moved toward the basket and, apparently, he spotted Elliot Washington in the left corner, down by the baseline.

Elliot took the pass and launched the shot. I had hurried to the end of the bench, in that direction, and when the ball was airborne it appeared it was a center cut. It hit the bottom of the net after the horn had sounded and we had a 90-89 victory.

Kentucky blew us away in the finals, 80-54, after we had stayed with them through the first half. With all due respect to Coach Rick Pitino and his Wildcats, it was obvious our team didn't have much left after what we had been through in the previous two games.

We advanced to the NCAA Tournament as the fifth seed in the Southeast Regional. Our first round opponent at Riverfront Coliseum in Cincinnati was Stanford.

Our inside players banged around pretty good and we got an 80-75 victory over The Cardinal. "Spree" led us with 23 points. Robert Horry had 19. "Hollywood" had 16 and Cedric Moore, our junior center, had 12.

It was a nice victory, one I'll definitely cherish because it was my last one at Alabama.

In the second round, we were ousted by North Carolina, 64-55, and went home to start making plans for a next season that never came for me.

CHAPTER SEVENTEEN

A Long, Tough and Tiring Day

*University of Alabama basketball had a successful
run through the 1980s and early part of the 1990s*

People have asked me over and over again what I felt when I walked out of Coleman Coliseum on the afternoon I was relieved of my duties as University of Alabama basketball coach.

I'll have to tell you the same thing I've told others. I can't explain exactly what I felt because I was numb at the end of a long, tough, tiring and emotional day.

I didn't feel good, that much I know, because a person doesn't give 32 years of his life to one employer and then like being asked to leave.

But carrying the last box of my belongings that had been cleaned out of my office and walking toward the fairly loaded van in front of Coleman Coliseum was hard because I was leaving a job I cherished. I was about to drive away from it and into an uncharted future, which is unsettling.

I know the news media was there because I've been told there were pictures in the newspapers and on television screens.

Other than that, I can't tell you much at all. Not a day goes by that I don't think about that time in my life, truthfully not one, and the events don't get any clearer every time I consider them.

I'm not ashamed to say I sat on my patio at our house at NorthRiver Yacht Club for weeks with tears in my eyes thinking about the past. I'm not just talking about the immediate past, rather about the good times I've shared with you in this book — the players, the wins, the losses and the people I've met along the way. I was extremely thankful for the sweet memories.

While I've admitted making mistakes, I was upset I had been convicted in the public's eye of doing something I hadn't done. All parties in the legal settlement reached are required not to talk about the specifics of the case. I agreed to that, so I can't explain some things as clearly as I would like.

One thing I can say is a person in a situation like that can learn how to separate friends from acquaintances.

I'm talking about a friend like Stanley Viciglio, who invited me to play in the Alabama Sports Hall of Fame Golf Tournament only a few days after my dismissal. He said, "Wimp, I'm your friend and I'll always be your friend."

I'm thankful for a person like that. Believe me, there weren't many to be found at that time.

I'm talking about a friend like Jimmy Rane, the chairman of Great Southern Wood. He gave me a job for two years and it helped me get past the crossroads in front of me and, by all means, kept me busy so I wouldn't spend all of my time thinking about what had happened.

De Martenson, my lawyer, gave me moral support as much as professional services. The same is true with Charles Dodson and Jimmy Taylor.

I'm appreciative of the letters of support I received, with most of them from University of Alabama basketball fans, and I wish I could personally meet the good people who wrote them.

There are other people to thank. They know who they are and they know I'm appreciative.

There are acquaintances who bailed out. They know who they are, so it serves no purpose to provide examples.

But I'm not going to focus on negatives. Instead, I'm going to say how blessed I was to be at The Capstone for 32 years.

I hope *Plaid and Parquet* has provided you with some insight into my life.

And, by golly, I'm not going to end this book talking about a sad time in my life. That isn't the way I want to be remembered.

Instead, I'd like to be remembered as an intensely competitive person who loved University of Alabama basketball and the State of Alabama.

EPILOGUE

May the Laughter Continue Forever

The coach famous for his scowl can smile on
success and special memories through the years

I'm not ready for a rocking chair, where people sit and spin yarns about their lives.

But I do enjoy remembering fun times from the past, even if some are embarrassing.

So let's run through a few afterthoughts with the idea a man better be able to laugh at himself or he will surely be miserable much of his life.

My Little Pal Pretzel

For a long time Annette and I have had a Dachshund named Pretzel, a yelping little dog with enormous energy who loves to chase and retrieve a tennis ball.

We've always shared taking care of Pretzel and there have been times when that duty has been perplexing to me. For instance, consider the time Annette went out of town and left our dog with me. This was when we were living in Little Rock.

I went out to get the mail after picking up something in the pantry. Well, I came back inside, started watching television and realized Pretzel wasn't with me. I couldn't find her in the house and figured she had zoomed through the door and was outside.

It was a cold night and I started combing the neighborhood. I went to every house and told our neighbors I had lost Pretzel, that I had to find her. I was in a panicked condition because I love that dog so much.

The neighbors joined in the hunt. I was downright panicky, thinking I had lost a great little dog. I was afraid she had taken off toward the highway.

After hours of looking, I went back to the house, downright discouraged and fearing the worst.

Then I heard a yelp. Pretzel was alive, but I couldn't tell where she was. After listening more closely and following her bark, I found her in the pantry, where I had closed the door on her.

When the neighbors asked about Pretzel, I just told them I had found her on my way home. They were as relieved as me. I wasn't about to tell them they had spent two hours in the cold looking for a little dog I had locked in the pantry.

On another occasion, Annette had gone to a movie with her friends and I couldn't find Pretzel when I got home from work. Again, I thought she had run out when I opened the door.

I got in the car and started driving around the neighborhood. I was flashing on the bright lights and shining them everywhere. I rolled down the window and called her — "Pretzel ... Pretzel ... Come here, girl."

I couldn't find her and it was about time for Annette to come home. So I called Judy Morgan, her friend, on a car phone and told them I had lost Pretzel. I gave them the whole story about driving around the neighborhood.

Well, they got home and started looking around the house. Lo and behold, Annette got on the floor and looked under a couch.

There she was. Pretzel had gone after a tennis ball and had gotten stuck under there.

To this day, I never leave a tennis ball on the floor or any other place Pretzel can reach.

Please Take Me Fishing

After we left a small apartment on Wood Avenue in Florence, Alabama just after we were married, Annette and I moved into an upstairs apartment in North Florence. We had good friends who lived below us, Janice and Jack Lard, and Patsy and Charlie Burks. This was when I was working at Reynolds Aluminum during summer from midnight to eight o'clock in the morning.

I wasn't a great fishermen, to say the least, although I had done some fishing with my uncle.

One day the man who owned the apartment building, Mr. Gladney, asked me if I wanted to go fishing with him. I told him I'd love to go.

We went out in his boat and settled down under Wilson Dam, where the water was deep, the current was strong and big rocks were plentiful.

I was in the front of the boat throwing out and he was in the back of the boat throwing out. I attempted to make a long cast and, with too much lead in my line, I slung it and backlashed my tackle. It was an awful mess.

I turned around and discovered I had hooked Mr. Gladney in an eyelid. He was moaning — ooooh ... ooooh ... ooooh — and I didn't know what to do. We had to work like the dickens to get that hook out of Mr. Gladney's eye.

Well, the next weekend I was standing out in front of the apartment when Mr. Gladney came by with his boat and motor behind his truck.

Mr. Gladney just waved at me and rolled on.

One time after we had moved to Tuscaloosa I went fishing with

Jim Blevins in Eutaw. He's the former University of Alabama football player who died recently, a really nice guy.

We were bream fishing with crickets and I didn't have a container for them. So I put mine in a paper sack and every time I attempted to get one out about a dozen would fall onto the ground or into the water.

Those fish were feasting for free.

Anyway, I had to go to the bathroom. I left my pole in the water. When I finished taking care of business, I looked and, lo and behold, my pole was bent toward the water.

At last I had a fish, which was looking like a monster. But as I got to the pole and reached for it, I slipped and hit the ground.

The fish fell off the hook and swam away.

Just Call Me Mrs. Wimp

I mentioned earlier that I'm not very mechanically oriented, such as gifted when running a lawn mower. Well, I don't think too good under pressure, either, when it comes to household chores.

You'll know what I mean after hearing how I cleaned up a mess.

Annette had just had a rug we used in the kitchen cleaned, an expensive undertaking. She went to play bridge one night in Little Rock and I was at the house by myself. So I decided I'd heat and eat a big bowl of chili.

I got it heated in the microwave and when I tried to get it out, it was so blooming hot I couldn't make it to the table. Splat — there went the chili, beans and all, all over that pretty rug.

I didn't know what to do. Finally, I decided to get the vacuum cleaner.

Obviously, you can't get chili up with a vacuum cleaner. Not only does it smear the beans and meat, it drives them deeper into the fabric. It isn't good for the vacuum cleaner either, as you might suspect.

I can't remember what Annette said when she got home that night, discovered the mess and heard my story about the big bowl of chili that got away. But I can remember the horrified look on her face before it was replaced with riotous laughter.

Annette spread the word, too, and I was the most embarrassed person in the world when our neighbors talked about that episode. To this day, many of those people still want to hear about the chili on the rug and the vacuum cleaner driving it in deeper.

C.M. Newton still remembers the afternoon he telephoned the house, just on a whim, and asked me what I was doing.

"I'm not doing anything," I said.

"No, really, what are you up to today?" C.M. said.

"I told you I'm not doing anything," I said.

C.M. knew something was up, so he kept pressing me to answer the question.

Finally, I said, "Okay, C.M., I'm ironing clothes."

"What?" C.M. said. "What are you really doing?"

"I'm ironing clothes," I said. "I noticed some clothes needed ironing and I started ironing. I'm still ironing."

I'm not sure C.M. ever believed I was ironing clothes. But I heard about it from a lot of people after confessing to him.

As I've told you, Annette and I had a hard time making ends meet for several years after we were married. I sort of figured the problem was her management of our finances, which has always been her responsibility because I'm so inept at it. So I told her I was going to take charge and start writing the checks, that we were spending too much on foolish things. I told her we were doing better than she thought and I would prove that to her. Reluctantly, she allowed me to take a shot at it.

I gathered up all of our bills, got the checkbook and went to the office so I could work in a quiet environment. After a short time, I had the bills paid, all of the checks written, and I went home excited.

I said, "Look, Annette, I've paid all of the bills and we've got a little left over. Like I said, you've been doing this all wrong."

Annette thought for a few minutes. Then she said, "Winfrey, I don't understand how that could be the case. Are you sure you paid everybody?"

"Absolutely," I said.

Then Annette said, "Did you pay the rent?"

"Oh, my gosh."

Now people who might wonder realize why most checks that come out of the Sanderson household have an Annette Sanderson signature on them.

I'm Not Much Of A Traveler

Coaching basketball has enabled me to do a lot of traveling, at times overseas, such as the time my friend Dave Odom and I got to go to Germany to do some clinics. We wanted to go to Paris for a day, so he and his wife, Annette and I and another couple drove over there in a VolksBus.

Dave was driving and I was riding shotgun. He pulled into a service station and said, "Wimp, we need to put some gas in this thing."

I jumped out of the bus and filled up the tank. Just as I finished, a guy came rushing out of the service station screaming in an unknown tongue, French, I guess, and he was all out of sorts. After a little interpretation and charades, I understood that I had filled up the bus with diesel fuel, not gas, and it wouldn't run a lick.

I asked the guy to syphon the diesel fuel out with his mouth. I couldn't believe it, but he tried to do that. But that was impossible, not a whole tank.

So we sent the VolksBus to Avis Rental and hiked around Paris all day.

To this day, Dave blames me for messing up and I blame Dave for putting such an important duty in the hands of a man who barely knows the difference between carburetor and tail light.

Some of the more enjoyable trips I've made were made possible by Jimmy Rane, the Auburn University Board of Trustees member and owner of Great Southern Wood or Osmose Lumber. When I was coaching at Alabama, he hired me to do some advertising for his company. Then after I was asked to leave

Tuscaloosa, he employed me for two years, until I took the job coaching at Arkansas Little Rock.

Jimmy is a wonderful man, a close friend, and I promise you he can organize some wonderful trips.

The last week in June is normally the time Jimmy gets together a group of coaches or former coaches for his trips. We started going to Alaska every year to fish for salmon. This year, 2000, we visited the "badlands" of the Wild West, principally Montana and Wyoming.

There are a million memories from those outings, some I'd like to share with you because there were some familiar names in the travel groups.

I've told you I'm an inexperienced fisherman, or not much of one at all. But I haven't told you how tough excursions in the deep sea can be on me.

We were in Alaska trying to catch salmon and halibut. Jimmy was there, of course, with his father and his brother. So were "Bebes" Stallings, the former Alabama football coach, Ray Goff, the former Georgia football coach. Cliff Ellis, the Auburn basketball coach, Pat Dye, the former Auburn football coach, Larry Blakeney, the Troy State football coach and several Osmose Lumber executives and guests.

We got on three or four small boats, went out as far as we could go, fished four or five hours, started back in, fished a few more hours and returned to shore. That made for some long days, no doubt, time that could have been shortened if we had rented a float airplane.

By the time we started toward shore, we were exhausted and most of us stretched out on the bottom of the boat to rest. The waves and bumps were awful, as bad as I've seen. I stood up to go to the front of the boat and we hit a bump, a bad one. My feet flew out from under me, I went up into the air and I came down with a thud on my hip and skidded across the bottom of the boat.

The next morning I told the coaches I was going to see Jimmy and beg him to let us get a float airplane to take us out and bring us back. I remember telling him, "Jimmy, I don't care how much it costs because I can't take another day like the first one."

There were some fishermen in that group, good ones, and I wasn't one of them. But everybody agreed I made a good contribution when I convinced Jimmy to hire a float airplane.

That was good for another reason, too, because we had some folks who got seasick, me included. Pat Dye usually got a little nauseated. I always got a whole lot nauseated.

A couple of years ago, I got deathly sick while we were fishing for salmon in Alaska. Blakeney and Goff were on the boat with me. I remember the captain asking if we wanted to turn back. Immediately, they said no, keep going deeper so we can fish for some halibut.

Trying to be funny, Larry and Ray tried to feed me a cigar minnow sandwich. That was it. I started throwing up — all over the deck, all over the bathroom and all over the walls. I felt like death eating a cracker.

Speaking of eating, University of Georgia Athletics Director Vince Dooley used to make trips with us. Normally, he lived up to his reputation, which went, "He would eat everything in sight, especially if it was free." The other guys got a kick out of me suggesting to the owners of the Red Fox Inn, a great restaurant, that they should hire an additional chef because Vince Dooley was on his way.

It was all in good fun, which is the way things are on those trips. I took a lot of ribbing and I handed out a lot. The same could be said for everybody else because we were from similar backgrounds and nobody was immune to problems of some type.

I'm sort of an instigator, I guess, and got another enlightening conversation going between two men who really don't have similar backgrounds. This one came several years ago, when "Bebes" Stallings was coaching at Alabama.

Joe Fine, the University of Alabama Board of Trustees member and a dear friend of Jimmy Rane, was on that trip. It came at a time when Crimson Tide fans were upset at "Bebes" for not passing the football much when he had Homer Smith as his offensive coordinator. I can't recall the year. But I'm sure Alabama fans can with ease because it was quite a controversy because the news media wouldn't let go of it.

Anyway, I took Joe Fine aside in a dining room and suggested he go ask "Bebes" why he refused to pass the football. Joe looked at me peculiarly and said, "Do you think that's an appropriate thing to do?" I told him I was sure "Bebes" and everybody else would get a good laugh from it. Frankly, I wasn't sure that was the case, but I knew "Bebes" had a good sense of humor and thought it'd be an interesting exchange to hear.

Joe took the bait and asked the question at the dinner table.

I've never seen "Bebes" look so startled. Also, I couldn't hear what he told Joe. But that doesn't matter because I don't think I could've printed it in this book if I had.

The escapade this year was wonderful because the setting in the "badlands" was so different than Alaska. The travel party included Jimmy, his father, Tony, and his brother, Greg, Pat Dye, Tommy Tuberville, the Auburn football coach, Ray Goff, Larry Blakeney, "Bebes" Stallings, Frank Robertson, Don Lusk, Paul Gordon and Lowell Barron of the Auburn Board of Trustees.

We flew into Rapids City, South Dakota, with the exception of "Bebes". He took a commercial flight and met us there. When he got off the airplane he had on a coat and tie, if you can believe a guy from Paris, Texas would show up in the Wild West dressed like that. I got on him hard and didn't let up.

Several days later, "Bebes" and I took a stroll around Cody,

Wyoming, looking at all the shops. It was a great visit with a longtime friend, as usual, and when we got on the bus with the other guys they got a kick out of me saying "Bebes" got upset because not one person in Cody, Wyoming recognized him.

One of the funny things that happened came after we flew into Jackson Ho, Wyoming. They have a place there called Billy's Hamburgers that served the hubcap variety. We knew Jimmy would want about six of them so we walked around the square for about an hour until the place opened.

I found a shop that specializes in unusual photographs. They let visitors dress up in western apparel, cowboy outfits, and take pictures. Well, we went in there and started pulling on the works, all the way down to suspenders. We looked like a bunch of gunslingers and the picture is included later in this book.

I'll leave it to you to pick out who is who in that portrait — and I'm betting you'll have trouble doing that.

My Actions Can Be Comical

There have been times when I've gotten a little too upset at my players for my own good. If you doubt that, consider this story Gary Waites, one of our super guards, likes to tell while laughing all the way through it.

We were playing Georgia and were behind at the half. In my estimation, we had played poorly and I planned to let our players know how I felt.

They were in the dressing room waiting for me to arrive, definitely fearing a tongue lashing.

I roared through the door and, in an effort to get their attention, hurried to a Gatorade bucket sitting in the middle of the dressing room. Thinking it was empty and would fly across the floor, I gave it a powerful kick. Instead, it was full of Gatorade and ice and the moment I hit it I knew I was in trouble.

The pain ran all the way up my leg and Gary says all of the players could see it mirrored on my face. I couldn't see them because my eyes were squinted, but he said they were shaking their heads and biting their lips to keep from laughing at me.

Somehow, we came back and won the game, which made my severely sprained big toe feel a little better. But the next day I limped to practice and had to sit and watch with my leg propped up with a bandage on my toe.

Henry "Sang" Lyda, our trainer, gave me an electrical device that was supposed to shock my toe into feeling better. But I spent much of that practice screaming at him because the shock was too hot and yelling at my players in an effort to get them to work hard on the court.

There was another time I embarrassed myself in the dressing

room, only that episode occurred during preseason practice at Coleman Coliseum.

We had chairs in the dressing room lined up so I could talk to our players like they were in a small classroom.

Well, practice had been terrible that day and I wanted to let them know how I felt.

As many people know, the mouth can get dry when a person has been working hard and the so called "cotton mouth" can get worse if a person is upset.

I was ranting and shaking my head when a wad of spit flew out of my mouth and hit Keith Askins squarely on his nose. Splat. Making matters worse, it stuck there and looked like a white pimple.

Keith knocked it away as quickly as he could, but that was it for the motivational talk. The players started laughing so hard they were about to cry.

I've been told they talked about that embarrassing moment all season — and some still do.

Speaking of Keith Askins, he still makes fun of me for another kicking episode after a road game we lost.

Normally, our players were provided boxed dinners after games and the food was sometimes delivered to the dressing room so they could eat on the bus going back to the hotel or to the airport.

On that evening I had jumped my players just after the loss but hadn't completely spoken my peace. So I went in to bend their ears a little more, got overly excited and kicked a big container with the boxed dinners in it.

I don't know if you've ever tried to romp around a room with a foot stuck in a boxed lunch, but I can tell that isn't easy to do.

Fore ... Fore ... Fore — Fire

If there is a passion in my life that matches my love for basketball, it's my love for golf. Also, that affection has led to one of my greater disappointments in life because I've never been able to master that sport to the point where my ability doesn't leave me embarrassed from time to time.

I don't imagine there's anybody in the world who has had as many lessons as I've had or anybody who has studied the mechanics of the golf swing as thoroughly as I have. I don't think anybody has looked at as many tapes as I have or has been taped as many times as I have. In summary, I doubt there's anybody who has had as much quality instruction as I have and still can't play a lick.

I'm still frustrated and bewildered because I can't play golf as well as I want to, for some reason not even good enough to be competitive.

But that doesn't mean I haven't had some great experiences on the golf course and continue to do so.

For instance, I used to play a lot during my years in Tuscaloosa with Jim Bates, his son Todd Bates and Henry "Sang" Lyda at Woodward Country Club and Frank House Golf Course outside Bessemer. We had some great games and a lot of fun.

One of the funnier experiences came when we had a match for a couple of dollars. Jim and I were partners and were going against "Sang" and Bobby Williams. As an exception to the rule, I was on the green on a par five in two or three shots and the guy I was playing against was in the woods after two shots. Without a doubt it looked like we were going to win the hole.

Well, lo and behold, Bobby Williams, the guy in the woods, smacked the ball and it moved toward the hole. But it was really moving and had no chance of going in, except for a big grasshopper jumping up and down on the green. The ball hit the grasshopper, bounced off and rolled into the cup.

Bobby Williams got an unbelievable eagle because of a grasshopper and got into my wallet. Also, he got a nickname, Grasshopper, that stuck with him.

Now you can see what type luck I have on the golf course.

I've told you about excursions with Dick Zeanah, Harry Cole, Paul Boschung and Bill McGuire to Willow Point near Alexander City, Alabama. But I haven't told you about the afternoon I was actually scoring well.

We were on the 17th hole and I hit my drive into the rough. Generally, I would hit another drive and go on. But I was playing good that day and wanted to complete the score. Much to the chagrin of my friends, I refused to quit looking for my ball.

Well, they played on without me and I stayed out there for more than hour looking for the ball. Then, alas, I found it and completed the hole by myself. Then I played the 18th hole and returned to our cabin.

The others were playing gin rummy when I walked into the cabin. Dick looked up from his cards and said, "Wimp, what did you have?" I told him I had two bogeys. In a snap, he said, "Buddy, if I had stayed out there for an hour and a half looking for a lost ball, I guarantee you I would've reported two pars."

Now you can see how precious a decent round is to a hacker like me.

Back in the good ol' days, the University of Alabama Athletics Department had an annual golf outing in Panama City, Florida for all of the coaches. At the time, an assistant coach for football was Bud Moore, who went on to become head coach at Kansas.

Bud, who is lefthanded, sliced a drive into a dump truck full of sand that was sitting on the left side of the fairway. The driver didn't know the ball was in the back, so after all of the tee shots were hit he continued his work. He drove to the green on the hole we were playing and dumped the sand near it.

When Bud got to the green, he looked and his golf ball was on the ground beside the pile of sand. For many years I've told people I was there when Bud Moore had the longest tee shot in the history of golf.

For a guy who hasn't been able to play well, I've had some great opportunities in golf. Thanks to some nice people, I've played some great courses, like Pebble Beach, Cypress Point, The Olympic Club, Firestone and, by all means, Augusta National.

The trips to The Olympic Club and Cypress Point, which is probably the most exclusive club in the United States, came about because I had coached Alabama in the Cable Car Classic Tournament in San Francisco. They invited me to come back for a few rounds of golf in the Bay Area, which was I tickled silly to do.

It was exciting playing The Olympic Club because of its proud U.S. Open tradition. That was about the extent of my thrill until I parred the final hole, where so much drama in pro golf has transpired.

The first hole at Cypress Point was the most compelling. It was a misty morning and I was assigned an older caddy who had obviously seen and heard a lot on that great golf course.

Well, we went to the first tee and I was extremely nervous. Wham. I hit my drive about a hundred yards into the heavy and wet rough. I hit my second shot into the fairway, but nowhere near the green. I hit my third shot over the green and into a sand trap. Then I took the sand wedge and hit the ball into the hole for an easy par four.

I was grinning, at least the best I can, when I looked at my experienced caddy and saw him scratching his head after witnessing four excruciating golf shots.

I'll always be indebted to Joe Ford, an Arkansas native and a member at Augusta National, for inviting me to play a round on the golf course that hosts the Masters. Another invitee was Bobby Knight, the Indiana coach.

I had been to Augusta to watch the Masters and had always wondered what it would be like to play there. Well, now that I've done it, I'd call it exciting and nervewrecking.

I was shaking on the first tee. I don't recall the specifics, but I had a double or triple bogey. In fact, I didn't have my first par until the 12th hole.

Of course, that's Golden Bell, the tricky, normally windy par three in the middle of fabled Amen Corner, so at least I had something to talk about after the round was over.

I don't think Joe Ford realizes the thrill he afforded me when he offered that invitation. The same is true with Dr. Jim Andrews, the famous orthopedic surgeon from Birmingham, Alabama, who has invited me several times to play at Firestone Country Club in Akron, Ohio.

Another great thrill for me was having the chance to participate in the Bruno's Memorial Classic during the spring of 2000 at Greystone Country Club near Birmingham, Alabama. That's where the top senior pros play each year.

I always knew my golf handicap, which is between 14 and 18, was not good enough for me to be invited to participate in a Bruno's Pro-Am Event, but for a long time I had hoped to be asked to appear in one. Quietly, I even dreamed about the chance while I was coaching basketball.

That's why I was so excited when Gene Hallman, who runs the tournament, invited me to participate.

Gene called and asked if I would be interested in participating in a "shootout" skins game in which two foursomes would play for up to $25,000 for charity. He told me he wanted me to be the amateur on one team, with three pros on my side, and Al del Greco, the Tennessee Oilers placekicker, to be the amateur on the other side with three pros.

I told Gene I'd love to do that, but that I didn't play well and he might want to invite somebody else. He said I was the invitee as long as I had a 15 handicap. I was at 16 at the time, probably higher now, but I accepted.

I worked on my game like crazy for a couple months and thought I might be getting better. But a few days before the "shootout" I played an easier course and had enough double bogeys to fill up a golf cart twice. Immediately, I telephoned Gene and told him he better find somebody else, that I didn't want to embarrass him, the Bruno's Classic and myself. He told me I had to play, that it had already been publicized.

Well, the day of "shootout" arrived and as soon as Sonny Smith and I ended our radio show at Greystone Country Club, I went to the practice tee and hit golf balls until my hands were about to bleed. I was scared to death.

My partners were Larry Nelson, the defending champion, Andy North, twice a U.S. Open winner and Allen Doyle. Al del Greco, who is good enough to be a pro, had Hubert Green, George Archer and Dana Quigley. I was overmatched, for sure, and on the first tee I begged Gene to let everybody hit before me so a bunch of the crowd would disperse. Instead, he announced that I would hit first.

I saw Jimmy Bryan, a longtime sports writer at *The Birmingham News*, standing nearby. I walked over to say hello and he said, "Wimp, just try to get the ball airborne." That was the worst thing he could have said. My stomach was in knots. But I got it airborne and after praying all of the night previous, I played about as good as I can and enjoyed being around seven nice men.

Well, on the last hole, four players tied and it was announced all of us would have to hit a sand trap shot with the closest to the hole winning $3,000 for charity.

After everybody other than me had hit, the closest ball to the hole was about three feet away. I figured that would be good enough to win, but I still had to take a shot at it.

I dug in as best I could. I opened up the blade of the sand wedge. I made a good swing and the ball came to rest a foot and a half or two from the hole to win the money.

It was a thrill of a lifetime and I've bragged about it so much on our radio show that people are sick of hearing about it. But what the listeners don't understand is I'm living proof miracles can happen.

Now let's get back to the real world with a couple more stories that are more revealing about my golf game.

Back in the old days, I used to play with Jock Sutherland, another assistant coach at Alabama, and some other people at Tuscaloosa Country Club.

Jock likes to tell a somewhat embellished story about a par three hole I played. He said I hit my tee shot onto the roof of a house where a man was working, that the ball hit the man in the head with enough force that he fell to the ground. He said I was undaunted. He said I walked into the yard, saw the man knocked out in a flower bed, picked up my golf ball and said, "Is anybody else playing Titleist 3?"

That one was a little exaggerated.

But it is true that I bought an old golf cart with oversized tires on it and took it Tuscaloosa Country Club to use. I was proud of that thing, a status symbol of sorts. However, during the first round we used it , it caught on fire and looked like a tank with smoke bellowing from it.

It took us a while to put it out, using water and sand, and I was more than a little embarrassed by the attention.

But, hey, that says a lot about my life because I've been starting fires and putting them out for a long time now.

The Players' Forum

The first time I met Coach Sanderson was during a summer camp just outside Atlanta, Georgia. He didn't have on a plaid sport coat that afternoon, but I knew he was there and I sort of watched him while playing a game on the court.

After the game, he introduced himself to me at a water fountain in the lobby of the gym.

That was a thrill for me. Also, that's the moment I started believing I had what it takes to play basketball at the collegiate level.

I doubted my abilities before that meeting. But I figured if Wimp Sanderson thought enough of me to say he would be in touch at a later date that I was good enough to make it as a player.

— **Gary Waites**
Alabama, 1988-1991

The Players' Forum

It was a dream come true for me to get to play basketball for Coach Wimp Sanderson at the University of Alabama. Having grown up in the state, in the same town as former Crimson Tide player Terry Williams, and having watch Bobby Lee Hurt and Buck Johnson star like they did, that was what I wanted out of high school.

Coach Sanderson made our team like a family. He was a father figure for me. He taught me responsibility. He genuinely cared about all of his players.

I can go back to my first meeting with him and get across that point. He told me he wanted me to come to Alabama and that I would have the chance to prove myself. He never said I would play. He said if I worked hard and became as good as I could be, then I would get to play.

It was all about work. He made us work, but he sweated just as much as we did. He put everything he had into us winning SEC Tournament championships. He put everything he had into us winning every game.

I can see him now running off the court after a victory at Auburn, his arms waving over his head and his fists shaking as their fans threw cups at him.

Then there was the Plaid Palace, the nickname Coleman Coliseum got because Coach Sanderson wore plaid coats and we won championships. The students wore plaid and they had masks with his picture on them. The whole place really started rocking before games started, then it got wilder.

We had the parquet floor. There was excitement all about

Alabama basketball. He created that atmosphere. He would thank the students for coming out to support us and they would react wildly. Then the enthusiasm seemed to grow for the next game.

I played in the NBA, where the atmosphere is upbeat. But even after that experience, I know what we had at Alabama was special.

Now that Coach Sanderson has retired, I have a couple of questions for him.

I used to notice that even as he ranted in the dressing room or made a pregame talk to us that he would stop and pick up every speck of paper or lint on the carpet. Or he would rearrange things to get them in perfect order, like the eraser at the chalk board. All the while he never quit talking.

Why is he such a neatness nut?

Also, we used to go out to Coach Sanderson's house for dinner, a family outing, and I always wondered why he had a golf ball washer on his patio.

So, Coach Sanderson, now that I can play golf, too, when can we get in a round?

— Keith Askins
Alabama, 1987-1990

The Players' Forum

When I hear the name Wimp Sanderson, I think of one fine person and one great basketball coach. Also, I think about the man who was the real reason I went to the University of Alabama to play basketball. He wasn't my head coach, rather Coach (C.M.) Newton was, but I was closer to him than anybody else.

I guess Alabama was always the favorite during the recruiting process, but I considered Memphis State a little and Indiana a lot. I even went to visit Indiana and Coach Bobby Knight.

But Wimp had me, mostly because of mutual respect. He seemed to respect me and my mother from day one. I respected him from day one. Because of that we've always been close.

I've laughed a lot with Wimp about the recruiting process. He has a lot of good stories to tell about that. He said he had a hard time getting me to commit. He's right about that because I was leading him on, playing it for all it was worth. But once I did commit, I stuck with it and he appreciated that.

Wimp has always been one of my favorite people. He's a nice man and he's a funny man. But more than anything, he's an outstanding coach.

Hey, what else can be said about what he accomplished at Alabama during his time as head coach?

I knew he had what it takes to be a good head coach, but, man, he did things that surprised me. He got big, for real. He got larger than I ever imagined he would.

— **Reggie King**
Alabama, 1976-1979

The Players' Forum

There's a lot to remember when I reflect on my years playing basketball at the University of Alabama under Coach Wimp Sanderson. But it's easy to pinpoint one thing that really sticks out, the respect he had across the Southeastern Conference.

There aren't many coaches in the history of college basketball who have been applauded by rival fans, but Coach Sanderson is one of them. I can remember a lot of nights when fans in Lexington, Knoxville, Nashville and other places gave him nice ovations. Obviously, they liked his colorful ways and his intensity during games. In some cases they might have liked the way our teams played. I hope that's true.

I'll never forget a night in Lexington when Kentucky Coach Rick Pitino showed up wearing a blue plaid sport coat. It was obvious he was mimicking Coach Sanderson, which I've always considered a high form of flattery or a show of respect. When Coach Sanderson came out in his plaid sport coat, they gave him a standing ovation. I don't know how many people Rupp Arena seats, but they were loud and they were showing appreciation. It was an honor watching that. He made us proud.

Then there were our home games, when the Plaid Palace would rock. We'd come out for warmups and Coach Sanderson would go greet our students. He'd take a bullhorn in hand and fire them up. We were amused by that. We were motivated, too.

Everybody knows how competitive Coach Sanderson is, you know, the famous scowling face. But most people don't know how he became even more competitive during my freshman season. That was in 1988, just after the SEC regular season championship and the SEC Tournament championship, when we lost Derrick McKey because he turned pro after his junior year.

Coach Sanderson told us we might be in for a hard grind, that he was looking for some winners who'd work hard in practice and play hard in games. He said we could overcome the loss of "D" if we worked at it and held together.

We sort of went in the hopper that season. But we had some good moments because we did play as a team and we fought hard on the court. As it worked out, that set the stage for our famous Three-Peat Run through the SEC Tournament. We made it three straight championships my senior season and that was extremely exciting after my freshman season.

But Coach Sanderson was about much more than winning. He did things that didn't fall into the job description because he genuinely cared about his players.

If somebody got out of line, he'd call a one-on-one meeting in his office and talk about what was right and what was wrong and how what was wrong would hurt the team. He was a master at putting out fires before they got started good.

Also, he was a father figure. Let's face it, some of our players didn't come from two parent homes. So he was there to provide fatherly guidance when it was needed.

There wasn't a down side playing for Coach Wimp Sanderson. He knew the Xs and Os of coaching. But he was mentor for a lot of us in ways other than that.

— Melvin Cheatum
Alabama, 1988-1991

The Players' Forum

Coach Wimp Sanderson has been a major factor in my life and my career in basketball. Certainly I'm glad for all of the good things that have happened to him through the years.

As I reflect on where we started from as a coach and a player and where we ended up, with such mutual admiration, I'm a little shocked we've come so far.

During my freshman season Coach Sanderson and I had a conflict that led to a confrontation. He was hollering at me all the time, screaming about this and that during practice, and that really bothered me. He didn't think I was putting forth as much effort as I should.

One day he asked me what it'd take to get me to play harder. I told him I'd do better in practice and in games and if he'd quit hollering so much, that I wasn't the type person who responded to that type coaching. I told him I knew when I was doing my best and that I'd try to do that all the time.

I've always been that type person. I'm a low key guy. I don't have to be whooping it up and showing a bunch of emotion on the basketball court to play at my best. I wasn't that way in college. I'm not that way in the NBA.

From that day on Coach Sanderson and I had a much better relationship, one that developed into a really good one. I got better as a player and I think both of us were much happier.

I'm extremely appreciative of Coach Sanderson for what he did for me. I'm not sure I would have developed into the type player I am today without his guidance. I don't think anybody can question his abilities as a coach. After all, what he accomplished at

Alabama, his resume, speaks for itself.

I've been asked a lot what it was like to play for Coach Sanderson. People have seen his lively ways on the bench, if that's what you would call it, and they wonder what he was like to be around every day. I tell everybody the same thing, that the man they saw on television wasn't like the man we saw for hour after hour during a season.

Coach Sanderson was totally different at practice. He was softspoken, at least much of the time, businesslike, and he worked hard to get us ready to play games. The animated man came to life when the lights came on.

In summary, Coach Sanderson is a great man with a great family. In fact, when I went back to Tuscaloosa for The Legends Weekend we had a couple of years ago, I was probably happier to see Mrs. Sanderson again than I was Coach Sanderson.

— Derrick McKey
Alabama, 1985-1987

The Players' Forum

When I first got to the University of Alabama, during the fall of 1982, I was a little uneasy around Coach Sanderson. He was an extremely intense individual and, frankly, I wasn't that good of a player. I might have been a little intimidated by him.

But now I call him a friend and we've got an extremely warm relationship that started developing in a most unusual way.

After my second season, Coach Sanderson called me into his office and, in essence, said I'd never be good enough to play at Alabama. He suggested I transfer to somewhere like Troy State.

I told him I didn't want to do that, that I was staying and I'd start for him the next season. He sort of laughed. Obviously, he doubted that.

I went to work, really hit the weight room, and because Craig Dudley got hurt, I got to go into a game. I went on the court and I never went back to the bench.

I think Coach Sanderson liked that type determination. I think that's where our special relationship got started.

I have great respect for Wimp Sanderson. I've been impressed by the way he took potentially good players and turned them into great players. He helped me develop. But I'm talking about people like Derrick McKey and Michael Ansley, real superstars.

More importantly, Coach Sanderson molded us into quality people. I'm convinced that's one reason we had so much success.

Then there were his unusual mannerisms.

Everybody knows about his competitiveness and how he got excited. But people don't know how he once kicked what he thought was an empty trash can in the dressing room at Auburn and ended up with a busted or badly bruised foot. He had a gosh awful expression on his face, a painful look, and it ruined his whole tirade.

Also, I got tickled by his country sayings. I'm talking about how he would watch a player having trouble shooting and say, "You couldn't put the basketball through there with a bow and arrow." If he thought you were questioning him or doing something you shouldn't be doing, Coach Sanderson would say, "Jim, I may have been born at night, but I wasn't born last night."

Then he always said things to motivate us that I suspected he made up. He'd read a newspaper article that said Charles Barkley said Auburn was going to kick us in the butt. Or he would talk about telephone calls and letters he received.

At the time, I think most of us believed him. Now I'm not so sure all he said was on the up and up.

Coach Sanderson did a great job with that program, turned into a bigtime winner and created excitement among students and other fans. I love the University of Alabama, but I don't think he was treated fairly at the end of his career there.

— Jim Farmer
Alabama, 1984-1987

Coach's Corner
A Final Word

I'm a fortunate person because I've gotten to know a side of Wimp Sanderson most people haven't met. I'm talking about the nice guy with the quick wit, something much more than a man in a plaid coat stomping his feet with a frown on his face.

Of course, now that you've read *Plaid and Parquet,* you should know more about that side of him.

Wimp and I became friends in the lobby of the Sandestin Hilton hotel in 1986, when my wife Diann and I arrived for our first SEC Spring Meeting. To be honest, I was apprehensive about being around high powered coaches, athletics directors and school presidents for the first time in that type of environment, so I was relieved when I saw his familiar face just after our arrival.

Not long after we got in our room that day, the telephone rang. It was Wimp, who said, "Richard, Annette and I would like for you and Diann to have dinner with us tonight."

Now, more than 15 years later, Wimp and I have a wonderful friendship that survived when we coached and recruited against each other when I was at Mississippi State and he was at Alabama. Isn't it wonderful a couple of guys can have a quick conversation, share a meal and develop that type of relationship?

Thank goodness Wimp noticed how nervous I was at that first SEC Meeting and placed that telephone call — and, believe me, that's the type person he is and always has been.

That dinner invitation shows what a caring compassionate person Wimp really is. After all, he was up and running at Alabama at that point, a regular in the NCAA Tournament, and he certainly didn't have anything to gain by trying to put me at ease.

That's why I value our friendship. That's why Diann and I think the world of Wimp and Annette, his lovely wife.

We've shared a lot of dinners since that first one, most of them with Diann and I laughing throughout about something Wimp said or did.

Also, Wimp and I have spent countless hours talking about basketball — actually, he talked and I listened — and we argued over wins and losses, most of them games his teams won.

I was upset when Wimp got out of coaching in 1992. I was delighted he would take the time to drive to Starkville, Mississippi to watch our Mississippi State teams practice and play. He even gave me input into things we were doing well and things we weren't doing so well.

I was glad to see him, as is always the case, but I had no idea he was preparing a scouting report on those visits to our practices and games. For you see, in 1996, the year Mississippi State made it to the Final Four, Wimp brought one of his Arkansas-Little Rock teams into Starkville and beat us.

I won't thank Wimp for giving me a coaching lesson that night.

But I am thankful he's a sincere and loyal friend who has given more to our friendship than I ever could.

— Richard Williams
Former College Basketball Coach

Wimp

Through The Years

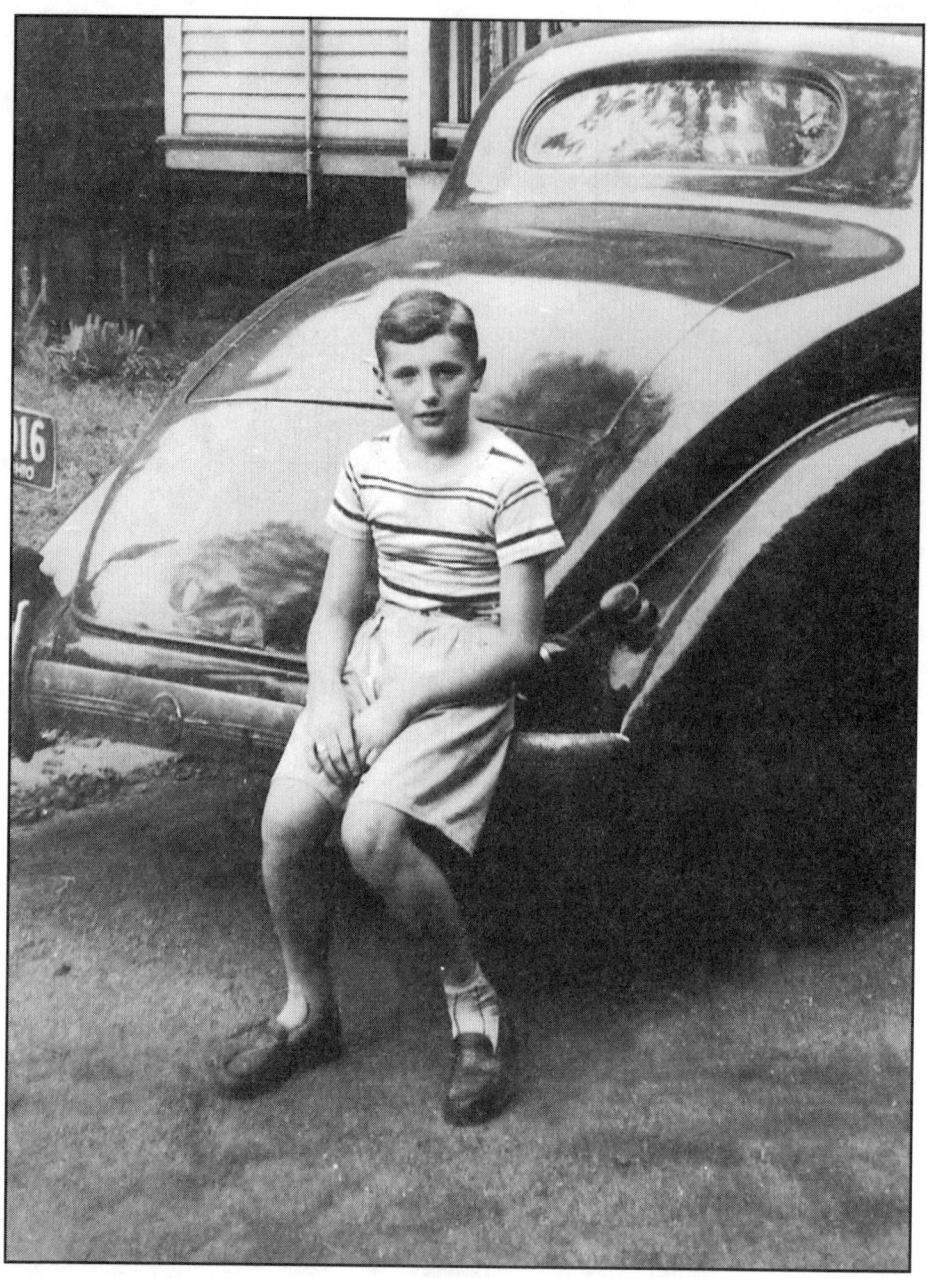

Wimp in Cleveland, Ohio as a child.

Wimp's
devoted mother,
Christine

Wimp and his father

*Wimp in famous
Black Snakes sweater*

Wimp as a college player

Wimp and Annette,
a young couple

Wimp, bottom left, played on a touring summer basketball team

Wimp and Dolly Parton, top left, Bill Walton, top right, Olivia Newton-John, bottom left, and Randy Owen.

Wimp and buddies on the "badlands" trip during the summer of 2000: top left to right, Greg Rane, Pat Dye, Don Lusk, Jimmy Rane, Lowell Barron, Wimp Sanderson, Frank Robertson, bottom left to right, Larry Blakeney, Tommy Tuberville, Tony Rane.

*Wimp and his
pal Pretzel*

Wimp, the frustrated golfer

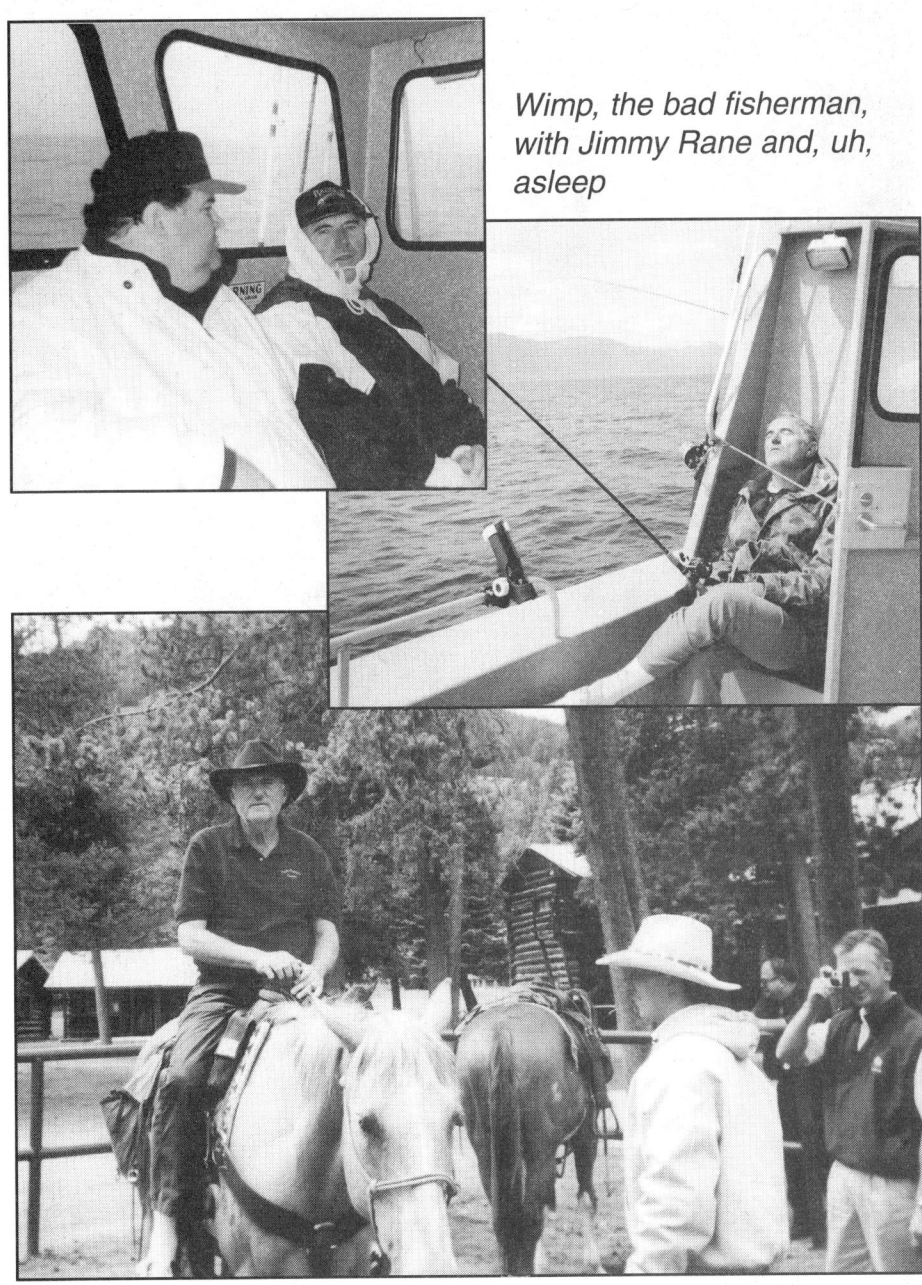

Wimp, the bad fisherman, with Jimmy Rane and, uh, asleep

Sitting tall in the saddle — a little slumped

That Unforgettable Face

On February 24, 1990, Wimp Sanderson was inducted into the Alabama State Sports Hall of Fame. His remarks on that occasion are on the following page.

"They wrote a song several years ago entitled *My Home's in Alabama*. I guess that sort of sums me up in one quick sentence.

"The important thing we must understand is what success we have belongs to others.

"In my case I am talking about the following people:

"My former players and assistant coaches ...

"Coach Ralph Smith, Coach Ed Billingham, Coach Hayden Riley and Coach C.M. Newton.

"Coach Paul Bryant and Coach Sam Bailey, who gambled on me.

"My family members ...

"My mom, Christine Sanderson, who kept me straight.

"Annette, Jim, Scott and Barry, who have endured 30 years of coaching.

"I asked Barry one time, after Jim and Scott had started coaching, why he wanted to coach. He said, 'Because the way I see it, you don't have to be too smart.'

"To those on the nominating and selection committee, I thank you for thinking of me.

"Lastly, each of us is interested in success ...

"How to attain it.

"How to handle it.

"How to retain it.

"Hopefully, I've learned all of these things.

"Thank you."

— Winfrey Sanderson
February 24, 1990